Words for Weeks 1–8

Week 1

- conceive
- inconceivable
- concept
- conceptualize

Week 2

- propose
- proposal
- proposition
- intend
- intention

Week 3

- exaggerate
- exaggeration
- minimize
- minimum
- minimal

Week 4

- unique
- identical
- dissimilar
- equivalent

Week 5

- narrate
- narrator
- narrative
- narration

Week 6

- demonstrate
- demonstration
- establish

Week 7

- trait
- characteristic
- character
- characterize
- property

Week 8

- option
- optional
- essential
- vital

conceive
DAY 1

(verb) To think up or form in the mind.

*Kari will **conceive** a plan to raise money for the new theater.*

inconceivable
DAY 2

(adj.) Impossible to believe or imagine.

*It was **inconceivable** to me that Luis would not tell the truth.*

concept
DAY 3

(noun) A general idea or thought.

*Fairness is a **concept** that most people understand.*

conceptualize
DAY 4

(verb) To form a concept or idea.

*When inventors **conceptualize** solutions to problems, they create new inventions.*

Day 1 conceive

1. How would you complete this sentence? Say it aloud to a partner.

I would like to conceive a way to ________.

2. Which word is a synonym for *conceive*? Circle your answer.

a. express
b. discover
c. think
d. build

3. Which skill or quality would help you *conceive* an idea for a science fair project? Circle your answer.

a. creative thinking
b. neat handwriting
c. good manners
d. a strong sense of smell

4. Describe a plan or idea you *conceived* with your friends.

____

____

Day 2 inconceivable

1. How would you complete this sentence? Say it aloud to a partner.

It would be inconceivable to ask a friend to ________.

2. Which word is an antonym for *inconceivable*? Circle your answer.

a. impossible
b. believable
c. unthinkable
d. incredible

3. Imagine a writing assignment where you are asked to create a fantasy character. List three qualities or physical traits that would make the character seem *inconceivable.*

a. ____

b. ____

c. ____

Day 3 concept

1. How would you complete this sentence? Say it aloud to a partner.

A concept I find hard to understand is ________.

2. Which sentence does not use *concept* correctly? Circle your answer.

a. Matt understands the concept of energy.
b. Angela's concept of fun is anything to do with sports.
c. We discussed several concepts in science class.
d. You can concept gravity by dropping an object.

3. Which word does not fit the usual *concept* of friendship? Circle your answer.

a. respect
b. loyalty
c. honesty
d. selfishness

4. Do you understand the *concept* of academic vocabulary? What is it?

____

____

Day 4 conceptualize

1. How would you complete this sentence? Say it aloud to a partner.

A job that might require being able to conceptualize is ________.

2. Imagine you were working to *conceptualize* a new invention. Which step would not be a logical part of the process? Circle your answer.

a. You come up with an idea in your mind.
b. You write the idea down on paper and try to work out the details.
c. You look for the invention you need in a book or on the Internet.
d. You see a need for a new invention.

3. Which of these would help you most when you need to *conceptualize* an idea? Circle your answer.

a. being a clear thinker
b. being a neat notetaker
c. being a friendly person
d. being a careful speller

Day 5 **conceive • inconceivable concept • conceptualize**

Fill in the bubble next to the correct answer.

1. Which of these is not something that a person could *conceive?*

Ⓐ a story plot
Ⓑ a game idea
Ⓒ an escape plan
Ⓓ a live animal

2. Which word is the best synonym for *inconceivable?*

Ⓕ unbelievable
Ⓖ unusual
Ⓗ odd
Ⓙ typical

3. Which noun names a *concept?*

Ⓐ college
Ⓑ knowledge
Ⓒ professor
Ⓓ computer

4. Which sentence uses the word *conceptualize* correctly?

Ⓕ Let's conceptualize our new friends after school.
Ⓖ We need time to conceptualize experience in science.
Ⓗ Sometimes it is easier to conceptualize a plan than to carry it out.
Ⓙ We were able to invent a new machine because we could not conceptualize.

Writing Describe your *concept* of the perfect school day. Use the word *concept* in your writing.

____

____

____

____

propose • proposal

DAY 1

propose

(verb) To suggest a plan or idea to be considered.

*Each member will **propose** a topic for the group project.*

proposal

(noun) A suggestion or plan.

*The group wrote a **proposal** to take a field trip.*

proposition

DAY 2

(noun) An offered or suggested plan of action.

*Enrique's **proposition** was that he would mow her lawn for a small fee.*

intend

DAY 3

(verb) To have something in mind as a goal, plan, or purpose.

*The students **intend** to raise money to pay for a class trip.*

intention

DAY 4

(noun) Something that you mean to do.

*The team's **intention** is to win the final game.*

Day 1 propose • proposal

1. How would you complete these sentences? Say them aloud to a partner.

When you propose an idea, it is important to ________.

I would like to make a proposal to my parents about ________.

2. Which word is a synonym for *propose*? Circle your answer.

a. accept
b. approve
c. require
d. suggest

3. Which sentence does not use *proposal* correctly? Circle your answer.

a. I need to do more research before I write my proposal.
b. Can you proposal a way to pay for new team uniforms?
c. Your proposal was the best idea of all.
d. The team's proposal was rejected by the coach.

4. If you were in charge of planning a class party, what would you *propose*?

____

____

Day 2 proposition

1. How would you complete this sentence? Say it aloud to a partner.

I think students in our school would support a proposition to ________.

2. Which of these would you not expect to find in a *proposition* to add more days to the school year? Circle your answer.

a. reasons for why more school days are needed
b. an explanation of the effect of having more school days
c. reasons for why there are already too many school days
d. suggestions for specific days to add to the school year

3. Which of these sentences are *propositions*? Circle your answers.

a. I'll do the dishes for three days if you let me go to the movie.
b. We can go to the pool on Saturday, and I'll teach you how to swim.
c. The last thing I did this morning was brush my teeth.
d. Dogs are very loving pets.

Day 3 intend

1. How would you complete this sentence? Say it aloud to a partner.

After school today, I intend to ________.

2. Match the person with the thing that he or she might *intend* to do. Write the correct letter on the line.

___ runner	a. publish a book of stories
___ postal worker	b. appear in a musical
___ singer	c. win a big race
___ writer	d. finish delivering mail by 3:30 p.m.

3. List three goals that you *intend* to meet this year in school.

a. ____

b. ____

c. ____

Day 4 intention

1. How would you complete this sentence? Say it aloud to a partner.

My intention is to be the best ________ I can be.

2. Which word is a synonym for *intention*? Circle your answer.

a. goal
b. success
c. effort
d. achievement

3. Which of these is the most accurate statement about an *intention*? Circle your answer.

a. It is something that you plan to study in school.
b. It is something that you want to do.
c. It is something that only happens in stories.
d. It is something that you would do only if you had to.

Day 5 **propose • proposal • proposition intend • intention**

Fill in the bubble next to the correct answer.

1. Which sentence uses both *propose* and *proposal* correctly?

Ⓐ The propose went well, but the proposal was still rejected.
Ⓑ They liked the proposal after the propose.
Ⓒ You should proposal any ideas you want to propose.
Ⓓ Any ideas you propose should be explained in a proposal.

2. Which of these is not true of a *proposition*?

Ⓕ It is a type of plan.
Ⓖ It is usually a secret.
Ⓗ It can be accepted or rejected.
Ⓙ It makes an offer to be considered.

3. To *intend* means to ________.

Ⓐ plan to do something
Ⓑ work on something
Ⓒ show something
Ⓓ imagine something

4. Which sentence does not use *intention* correctly?

Ⓕ Our intention is to form a group of volunteers.
Ⓖ The intention of each volunteer is to help others.
Ⓗ We intention to work with children.
Ⓙ It is our intention to raise money for the school.

Writing *Propose* a new award for students in your school. Use the words *propose* and *proposal* in your writing.

exggerate • exaggeration

DAY 1

exaggerate

(verb) To make something seem larger, more valuable, or more important than it is.

*Drawings sometimes **exaggerate** the size of a shark's teeth.*

exaggeration

(noun) The act of exaggerating.

*It is an **exaggeration** to say that I can hit a ball clear into the next county.*

minimize

DAY 2

(verb) To make something as small as possible.

*We can **minimize** the amount of work for each student if we work together as a team.*

minimum

DAY 3

(noun) The smallest possible amount or lowest limit.

*One dollar is the **minimum** that you can donate to the fund.*

minimal

DAY 4

(adj.) Being the smallest in amount or size.

*It takes **minimal** effort to smile, but the rewards are big.*

Day 1 exaggerate • exaggeration

1. How would you complete these sentences? Say them aloud to a partner.

Something that people exaggerate about is ________.

An exaggeration might be, "My room is ________."

2. Which phrase describes what people do when they *exaggerate?* Circle your answer.

a. hide the truth
b. stretch the truth
c. discover the truth
d. tell the truth

3. Which of these is the best example of something that shows *exaggeration* in a story? Circle your answer.

a. a character with superhuman strength
b. a familiar theme, such as friendship
c. a plot with a surprise ending
d. a setting that takes place long ago

4. Write about a time you *exaggerated.*

____

____

Day 2 minimize

1. How would you complete this sentence? Say it aloud to a partner.

I think people should minimize ________.

2. Which sentence uses *minimize* correctly? Circle your answer.

a. Students can minimize the desks in their classroom.
b. Students can minimize the lunch period by eating slowly.
c. Students can minimize noise by speaking quietly.
d. Students can minimize their lockers by keeping them neat.

3. What is the result if your teacher agrees to *minimize* the amount of homework? Circle your answer.

a. You would get no homework.
b. You would get more homework.
c. You would get more time for homework.
d. You would get less homework.

Day 3 minimum

1. **How would you complete this sentence? Say it aloud to a partner.**

   The minimum amount of time I spend on homework is ________.

2. **Which word would you associate with the meaning of *minimum*? Circle your answer.**

   a. best c. less
   b. least d. worst

3. **A contest requires an essay that has a *minimum* of 200 words. Which of these would eliminate you from the contest? Circle your answer.**

   a. writing an essay of 200 words
   b. writing an essay of more than 200 words
   c. writing an essay of less than 200 words
   d. writing an essay with 200 words on each page

4. **If your teacher asks you to keep your talking to a *minimum*, what does that mean?**

   ____

   ____

Day 4 minimal

1. **How would you complete this sentence? Say it aloud to a partner.**

   ________ is an activity that used to be hard for me, but now it takes minimal effort.

2. **If a storm did *minimal* damage, which adjective would be best for describing the storm? Circle your answer.**

   a. huge c. major
   b. terrible d. mild

3. **Which of these would require *minimal* care? Circle your answer.**

   a. a cactus c. a baby
   b. a dog d. a horse

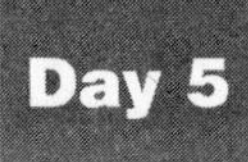

Day 5 exaggerate • exaggeration
minimize • minimum • minimal

Fill in the bubble next to the correct answer.

1. Which statement is correct?

Ⓐ An exaggeration is a made-up character.
Ⓑ To exaggerate means to tell a secret.
Ⓒ You cannot exaggerate when you talk.
Ⓓ An exaggeration can make something seem bigger than it is.

2. Which word is the opposite of *minimize*?

Ⓕ increase
Ⓖ improve
Ⓗ decrease
Ⓙ big

3. If you do the *minimum* on an assignment, which of these describes your behavior?

Ⓐ You do more than you need to do.
Ⓑ You do less than you need to do.
Ⓒ You do only what you are required to do.
Ⓓ You do only what you want to do.

4. Which adjective means the same as *minimal*?

Ⓕ slow
Ⓖ smallest
Ⓗ massive
Ⓙ small

Writing Write an *exaggeration* about a time you were hungry.

____

____

____

____

unique

DAY 1

(adj.) Being the only one of its kind.

*The painting is **unique** because it is the only one by this artist.*

identical

DAY 2

(adj.) Exactly alike.

*No two days in school are **identical** because something different happens each day.*

dissimilar

DAY 3

(adj.) Not alike; different.

*Even though they are twins, the girls are **dissimilar**.*

equivalent

DAY 4

(adj.) The same as, or equal to, another thing.

*The winter break from school is shorter than summer vacation. They are not **equivalent**.*

Day 1 unique

1. How would you complete this sentence? Say it aloud to a partner.

Something that makes me unique is ________.

2. Which word is an antonym for *unique*? Circle your answer.

a. different
b. common
c. unusual
d. ugly

3. The teacher says that your topic for the science report is *unique*. What does that mean? Circle your answer.

a. Several other students have chosen the same topic.
b. Your topic has been done many times in the past.
c. You have the best idea for a topic in the class.
d. You are the only student who thought of that topic.

4. What is something you have that is *unique*?

____

____

Day 2 identical

1. How would you complete this sentence? Say it aloud to a partner.

A friend who had identical interests to mine would like ________.

2. Which sentence uses *identical* correctly? Circle your answer.

a. The elephant and giraffe at the zoo were identical.
b. The lockers are identical, with different colors and sizes.
c. Our reading books are identical, so everyone has the same stories.
d. Many sports are identical because they all use a ball.

3. Which word is a synonym for *identical*? Circle your answer.

a. matching
b. similar
c. interesting
d. special

Day 3 dissimilar

1. How would you complete this sentence? Say it aloud to a partner.

Two dissimilar interests I have are ________ and ________.

2. If two books are *dissimilar,* which statement is probably true about them? Circle your answer.

a. They are written by the same author and have the same characters.
b. They are the same book, but one is an older copy.
c. They are on different topics and written by different authors.
d. They are on the same topic and have the same number of pages.

3. Which word would not describe two people who are *dissimilar?* Circle your answer.

a. same
b. opposite
c. different
d. unlike

4. Can two people who are *dissimilar* still be friends? Why or why not?

____

____

Day 4 equivalent

1. How would you complete this sentence? Say it aloud to a partner.

There is no school that is equivalent to ours because ________.

2. A writing partner suggests you change a word to one with an *equivalent* meaning. What kind of word do you need? Circle your answer.

a. a word with a different meaning
b. a word that is easier to understand
c. a word that has many meanings
d. a word with the same meaning

3. If two foods are *equivalent* in calories, which statement is true about them? Circle your answer.

a. One food is better for you than the other.
b. Both foods have an equal number of calories.
c. Both foods look and taste exactly alike.
d. Both foods are high in calories.

Day 5 unique • identical • dissimilar • equivalent

Fill in the bubble next to the correct answer.

1. A *unique* gift is ________.

Ⓐ one of a kind
Ⓑ attractive
Ⓒ easy to find
Ⓓ breakable

2. If two sounds are *identical,* they are ________.

Ⓕ quiet
Ⓖ loud
Ⓗ alike
Ⓙ distinctive

3. Two *dissimilar* sports ________.

Ⓐ use the same equipment
Ⓑ have the same rules
Ⓒ are unpopular
Ⓓ are different in many ways

4. If two sums are *equivalent,* they ________.

Ⓕ are both big numbers
Ⓖ are equal in value
Ⓗ are difficult to add
Ⓙ can be divided by 12

Writing What makes each person a *unique* individual? Explain your ideas. Use the word *unique* in your writing.

____

____

____

____

narrate

DAY 1

(verb) To tell the story or give an account of something in speech or writing.

*Each team member will **narrate** a portion of the presentation.*

narrator

DAY 2

(noun) A person or character who tells a story.

*The play has a **narrator** who introduces all the characters.*

narrative

DAY 3

(noun) A story, description, or account of events.

*The assignment was to write a **narrative** about your first day of school.*

narration

DAY 4

(noun) The act of narrating.

*The concert will include music and **narration** about the history of our country.*

Day 1 narrate

1. How would you complete this sentence? Say it aloud to a partner.

In order to narrate a story, I would need to ________.

2. A test question asks you to *narrate* an account of a memorable birthday. Which statement describes what you need to do? Circle your answer.

a. Write a description of what happened on a special birthday.
b. Analyze a reading passage about a special birthday.
c. Find the total cost of a special birthday party.
d. Think of a title for a story about what happened on a special birthday.

3. Which of these might you do if you were asked to *narrate* a presentation of a folk tale? Circle your answer.

a. be a character in the folk tale
b. introduce the characters of the story and describe the things they do
c. wait to see the movie based on the story
d. write another story

4. What is a story, play, or movie you would like to *narrate*?

____

Day 2 narrator

1. How would you complete this sentence? Say it aloud to a partner.

To do a good job as a narrator, you need to ________.

2. Which of these explains what the *narrator* of a movie does? Circle your answer.

a. makes the costumes for the characters in the movie
b. doesn't say anything
c. watches the movie
d. tells the audience important story details

3. Which type of story always has a *narrator*? Circle your answer.

a. an article that describes an important historical event
b. a story in which one character describes the action
c. a science fiction tale
d. a fairy tale

Day 3 narrative

1. How would you complete this sentence? Say it aloud to a partner.

A narrative about my typical school day would include ________.

2. You have an assignment to write a *narrative* about something you did with a friend. Which of the following would fit the assignment? Circle your answer.

a. a list of Web sites about friends
b. a report on what your friend looks like
c. a card that you would send to the friend
d. an account of the time you both camped out in the backyard

3. Which sentence uses *narrative* correctly? Circle your answer.

a. Each student will have a chance to narrative a story.
b. The narrative did not speak loud enough for everyone to hear.
c. Her narrative about her week at camp was as exciting as an adventure story.
d. The movie was hard to understand and needed a character to narrative.

Day 4 narration

1. How would you complete this sentence? Say it aloud to a partner.

Something that I recently saw or heard that had narration was ________.

2. Your teacher asks the class to write a *narration* for photographs of the class field trip to present to parents. What is the class doing? Circle your answer.

a. writing descriptions of the photographs to be read aloud
b. writing the names of everyone in the photographs
c. writing thank-you letters to the bus driver and tour guide
d. writing a list of facts students learned on the field trip

3. Which sentence uses *narration* correctly? Circle your answer.

a. You need a good voice to be a narration.
b. The play had a character who was the narration.
c. Many famous actors narration audiobooks.
d. The movie began with a narration that introduced the characters.

4. How would you prepare if you were to do a *narration* of a book?

____

____

Day 5 narrate • narrator • narrative • narration

Fill in the bubble next to the correct answer.

1. Which of these would you most likely be asked to *narrate*?

- Ⓐ the title of a book
- Ⓑ a list of things you had for lunch yesterday
- Ⓒ your home telephone number
- Ⓓ a story about something that happened to you

2. Which word is a synonym for *narrator*?

- Ⓕ librarian
- Ⓖ storyteller
- Ⓗ artist
- Ⓙ leader

3. Which word is not a synonym for *narrative*?

- Ⓐ account
- Ⓑ tale
- Ⓒ newspaper
- Ⓓ description

4. Which word explains the purpose of *narration*?

- Ⓕ telling
- Ⓖ seeing
- Ⓗ guessing
- Ⓙ hiding

Writing Explain some of the things you would include in a *narrative* about your favorite field trip. Be sure to include the word *narrative* in your writing.

demonstrate • demonstration DAY 1

demonstrate

(verb) To teach or explain by showing how to do or use something. *The coach will **demonstrate** the proper way to hold a bat.*

demonstration

(noun) An act of teaching, explaining, or operating something. *The health class will get a **demonstration** of how to clean a cut.*

demonstrate DAY 2

(verb) To prove or show clearly. *A capable lawyer will **demonstrate** her client's innocence.*

establish DAY 3

(verb) To prove or show something to be true. *The attendance count will **establish** that most students in our school are present today.*

establish DAY 4

(verb) To create or start. *The school will **establish** a new award to recognize good conduct.*

Day 1 demonstrate • demonstration

1. How would you complete these sentences? Say them aloud to a partner.

I can demonstrate how to ________.

I have seen a demonstration of ________.

2. Which of these are required to *demonstrate* how to paint with watercolors? Circle your answer.

a. a pencil and crayons
b. visits to an art museum
c. books about artists
d. a paintbrush and watercolors

3. Which of these would be a *demonstration* of what to do in a fire drill? Circle your answer.

a. A student refuses to get up from his desk.
b. A student writes a report on fire drills.
c. A student gets up from his desk and leaves the classroom in an orderly way.
d. A student shows the class that fire is dangerous.

4. What would you like to see a *demonstration* of?

____

Day 2 demonstrate

1. How would you complete this sentence? Say it aloud to a partner.

I can demonstrate that something floats by ________.

2. Which of these would <u>not</u> help you *demonstrate* that you are a responsible student? Circle your answer.

a. turning in homework on time
b. saying that you will be responsible from now on
c. obeying school rules
d. completing your share of a team project

3. Which of these would *demonstrate* that a team needs new uniforms? Circle your answer.

a. lots of rips and tears in the old uniforms
b. players who do not like the old uniforms
c. pictures of new uniforms
d. pictures of another team with new uniforms

Day 3 establish

1. How would you complete this sentence? Say it aloud to a partner.

I can establish that I am ________ by ________.

2. You are reading about how a scientist worked to *establish* a theory. What are you learning? Circle your answer.

a. why the scientist refused to believe the theory
b. how to write a science report
c. how the scientist built her lab
d. how the scientist proved the theory was correct

3. Which of these would best help you *establish* that you have musical talent? Circle your answer.

a. singing a song in the school concert
b. knowing the names of all the musical instruments in a band
c. listening to music every day
d. talking about music with your friends

Day 4 establish

1. How would you complete this sentence? Say it aloud to a partner.

One thing I can do to establish good study habits is ________.

2. A history test asks a question about efforts to *establish* the United States as a country. Which of the following is most likely to be the question? Circle your answer.

a. How did the United States come into being?
b. What is the present size and population of the United States?
c. How can you prove that the United States is a country?
d. What will the United States be like in 50 years?

3. Which of these would you <u>not</u> need in order to *establish* a new sports team at school? Circle your answer.

a. students who want to be on the team
b. trophies for outstanding players
c. equipment to play the sport
d. a coach for the team

4. What club, team, or activity would you like to *establish* at your school?

____

Day 5 demonstrate • demonstration • establish

Fill in the bubble next to the correct answer.

1. Which pair of words are both synonyms for *demonstrate?*

- Ⓐ see—hear
- Ⓑ prove—instruct
- Ⓒ hide—tell
- Ⓓ agree—refuse

2. In which sentence could *demonstration* be used to fill in the blank?

- Ⓕ A chef will ________ to show others how to cook.
- Ⓖ For our science project we can ________ how a battery works.
- Ⓗ The swimming coach is a good ________ for how to dive.
- Ⓙ A ________ will help us understand how to use the camera.

3. Which of these would *establish* that a school rule was broken?

- Ⓐ a list of school rules
- Ⓑ students who disagree with the rule
- Ⓒ proof that the rule was broken
- Ⓓ a student in the principal's office

4. To *establish* a rock-collecting club, you would need ________.

- Ⓕ friends who also enjoyed collecting rocks and wanted to join
- Ⓖ a lot of rocks in your backyard
- Ⓗ to show that there already was such a club
- Ⓙ to go shopping

Writing How can you *demonstrate* that you are a good friend to others? Use one of this week's words in your writing.

____

____

____

____

trait

DAY 1

(noun) A special quality or feature of a person or animal.

*Creativity is a **trait** that most artists have.*

characteristic • character

DAY 2

characteristic

(noun) A regular quality or feature of someone or something.

*Fast action is a **characteristic** of a soccer game.*

---

character

(noun) All of the many things that make one person or thing different from another.

*The parks and playgrounds in this neighborhood give it a friendly **character**.*

characterize

DAY 3

(verb) To describe the character and qualities of someone or something.

*You could **characterize** life in a city as noisy and busy.*

property

DAY 4

(noun) A distinctive physical characteristic of something; a common quality of all things belonging to a particular group.

*One **property** of oxygen is that it has no smell.*

Day 1 trait

1. How would you complete this sentence? Say it aloud to a partner.

One of my personality traits is ________.

2. Think of a character in a book you have read. What *traits* does the character have?

a. ______________________________

b. ______________________________

c. ______________________________

One of my most noticeable **traits** is my good looks.

3. Which word is a synonym for *trait*? Circle your answer.

a. personality
b. description
c. quality
d. sign

Day 2 characteristic • character

1. How would you complete these sentences? Say them aloud to a partner.

An elephant's characteristics are ________.

A principal's character is often ________.

2. Which sentence does not use *characteristic* correctly? Circle your answer.

a. Curly hair is a characteristic of some families.
b. Stripes are a characteristic of the zebra.
c. One characteristic of poetry is rhyme.
d. The person in the book was characteristic.

3. Think about your own *character.* What are three *characteristics* you can name?

a. ______________________________

b. ______________________________

c. ______________________________

Day 3 characterize

1. How would you complete this sentence? Say it aloud to a partner.

I would characterize my school as ________.

2. Which of these *characterizes* a poorly written paragraph? Circle your answers.

a. exciting language
b. many errors
c. no main idea
d. funny

3. What *characterizes* a good song? List three characteristics.

a. ________________________________

b. ________________________________

c. ________________________________

4. How would you *characterize* the last book you read? Complete the chart.

Good Characteristics	Bad Characteristics

Day 4 property

1. How would you complete this sentence? Say it aloud to a partner.

Some of the properties of modeling clay are ________.

2. Which of these things are *properties* of sugar? Circle your answers.

a. forms as crystals
b. dissolves in liquid
c. tastes bitter
d. wet

3. Which word is a synonym for the word *property*? Circle your answer.

a. characteristic
b. condition
c. chemical
d. difference

Day 5 trait • characteristic • character characterize • property

Fill in the bubble next to the correct answer.

1. Which sentence uses the word *trait* correctly?

Ⓐ A common trait of cats is curiosity.

Ⓑ A good friend has the trait of a nice home.

Ⓒ One trait of nurses is that they go to college.

Ⓓ The rock has the trait of being shiny.

2. Which of the following is not a common *characteristic* of a typical scientist?

Ⓕ intelligent

Ⓖ curious

Ⓗ careless

Ⓙ careful

3. Which sentence does not use the word *character* correctly?

Ⓐ A mother should have a kind and patient character.

Ⓑ One character of a guide dog is that it obeys its master.

Ⓒ The movie star's rude, unfriendly character won him no friends.

Ⓓ The room had a warm, inviting character.

4. Which sentence describes a *property*?

Ⓕ A property is an animal trait.

Ⓖ A property describes the character of something.

Ⓗ A property is always true and does not change.

Ⓙ A property describes a person's personality.

Writing How would you *characterize* the city or town where you live? Use at least one of this week's words in your writing.

option
DAY 1

(noun) One of several things that can be chosen.

*Pizza is one **option** for lunch today.*

optional
DAY 2

(adj.) Left to your own choice to do; not required.

*Attending school is not **optional** for most students.*

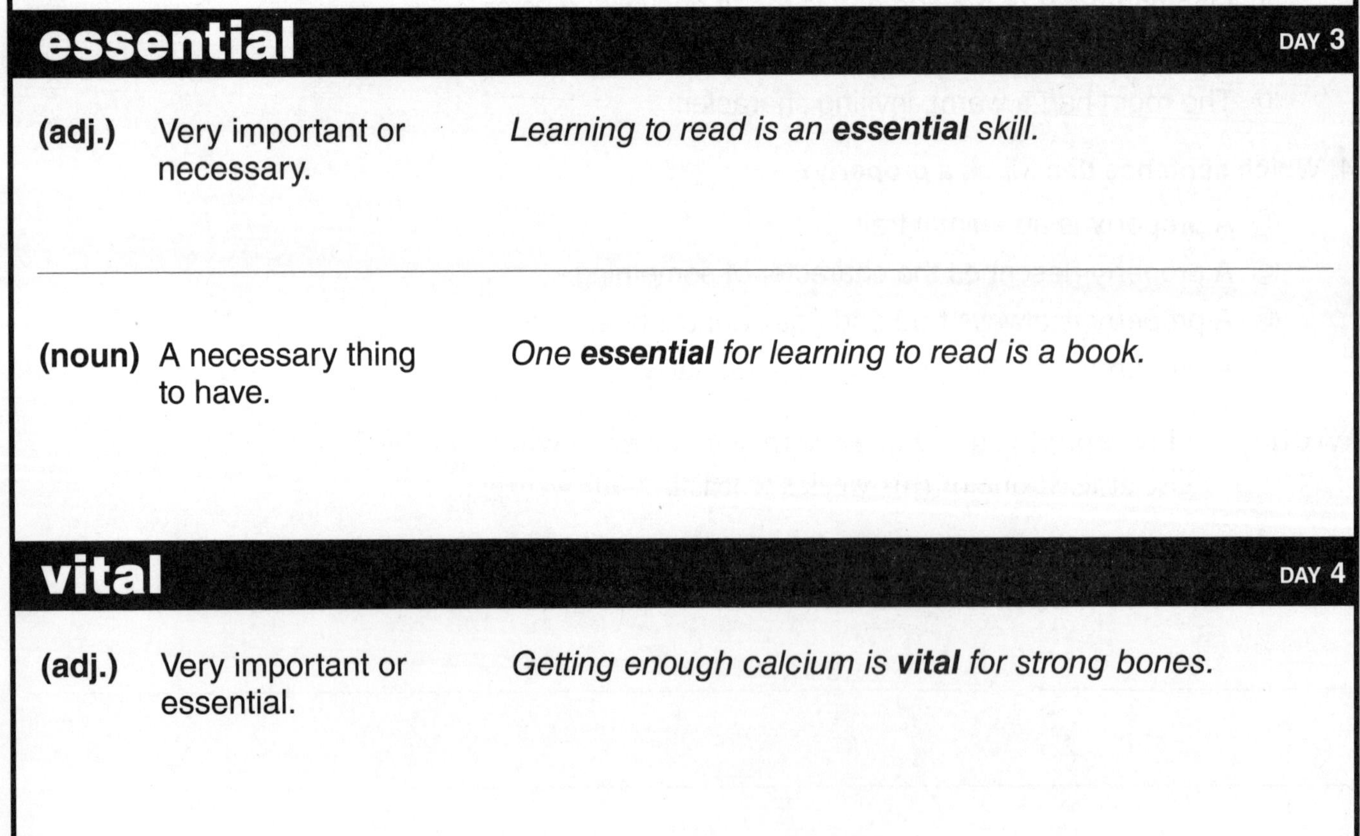

essential
DAY 3

(adj.) Very important or necessary.

*Learning to read is an **essential** skill.*

(noun) A necessary thing to have.

*One **essential** for learning to read is a book.*

vital
DAY 4

(adj.) Very important or essential.

*Getting enough calcium is **vital** for strong bones.*

Day 1 option

1. How would you complete this sentence? Say it aloud to a partner.

One option I always have for an after-school activity is ________.

2. Which word is a synonym for *option*? Circle your answer.

a. selection
b. choice
c. requirement
d. belief

3. What are your *options* of things to do this weekend? List three of them.

a. ____________________

b. ____________________

c. ____________________

Day 2 optional

1. How would you complete this sentence? Say it aloud to a partner.

One school subject that I feel should be optional is ________.

2. The teacher announces that today's quiz is *optional.* What does that mean? Circle your answer.

a. Everyone in the class must take the quiz.
b. Only some students in the class must take the quiz.
c. The teacher changed her mind about giving the quiz.
d. Each student can choose whether to take the quiz.

3. Which sentence uses *optional* correctly? Circle your answer.

a. Optional activities at camp are fishing and bird-watching.
b. We have one optional for a movie to watch tonight.
c. The optional question must be answered to complete the test.
d. The show was so optional that I couldn't stop laughing.

4. Which activities or subjects are *optional* at your school?

____

Day 3 essential

1. How would you complete these sentences? Say them aloud to a partner.

One of the essential things I do before school is ________.

Something that many kids consider an essential is a(n) ________.

2. Which adjective is a synonym for *essential*? Circle your answer.

a. flexible
c. exciting
b. critical
d. extra

3. Which objects are *essentials* in a classroom? Circle your answer.

a. posters
c. books
b. plants
d. aquariums

4. What activity is *essential* to you?

____

Day 4 vital

1. How would you complete this sentence? Say it aloud to a partner.

To be good at a sport, it is vital to ________.

2. Your teacher says the class will discuss *vital* events that are happening in the world today. What does that mean? Circle your answer.

a. The class will discuss every event in the history of the world.
b. The class will discuss the most important current world events.
c. The class discussion is an important event.
d. There are discussions happening in the world today.

3. Which word is an antonym for *vital*? Circle your answer.

a. essential
c. unnecessary
b. unusual
d. unhappy

4. What resources are *vital* for plant life?

____

Day 5 option • optional • essential • vital

Fill in the bubble next to the correct answer.

1. Which list gives several different *options* for ways to get home from school?

- Ⓐ a bus, a steering wheel, a seat
- Ⓑ a door, a window, the sidewalk
- Ⓒ a bus, a bicycle, walking
- Ⓓ a plane, an elevator, a shopping cart

2. In which sentence could *optional* replace the underlined word?

- Ⓕ Practice today is required for all team members.
- Ⓖ New uniforms are needed this year.
- Ⓗ The coaches have busy schedules this year.
- Ⓙ Attending the team dinner is voluntary this year.

3. Which sentence uses *essential* correctly?

- Ⓐ A passport is essential to visit another country.
- Ⓑ A stove is the essential that we don't need to have.
- Ⓒ We can essential food for a few days.
- Ⓓ I like to travel with my essential.

4. In which sentence could the word *vital* fill in the blank?

- Ⓕ The recipe will taste as good without that ________ ingredient.
- Ⓖ If that step is ________, we can skip it.
- Ⓗ Reading to the end is ________ for understanding the story.
- Ⓙ The plan was ________ and soon forgotten.

Writing What qualities or behaviors are *essential* for success in school? Include the word *essential* in your writing.

____

____

____

____

____

REVIEW: Weeks 1–8

characteristic	**dissimilar**	**establish**	**intended**	**narrative**
characterized	**essentials**	**inconceivable**	**minimal**	**vital**

Day 1

Fill in the blanks with words from the word box.

Can you imagine a place that receives less than one millimeter of rain a year? Such a place seems ______________________ because water is so necessary for life. Two-thirds of a human body consists of this ______________________ resource. But in the Atacama Desert in Chile, it rarely rains. The lack of water is the ______________________ that makes it the driest place on Earth. Rainfall is so ______________________ that in some parts of the desert there is no life. In fact, scientists have used the Atacama to ______________________ the smallest amount of water any life needs to exist.

Day 2

Fill in the blanks with words from the word box.

In class, we read a ______________________ by a girl named Zlata Filipovic. She kept a diary from 1991 to 1993 about her life in the Bosnian capital city of Sarajevo. Different groups of people with ______________________ beliefs were struggling to take control of the city at the time. Zlata described living in a war zone and ______________________ life as difficult and scary. Survival was challenged on a daily basis. People went for days without ______________________ such as food, water, and gas. Zlata's story is amazing. If my teacher ______________________ for us to appreciate our lives more after reading this, it worked!

REVIEW: Weeks 1–8

concept	**equivalent**	**intention**	**options**	**proposed**	**unique**
demonstration	**identical**	**minimum**	**property**	**proposition**	

Day 3

Fill in the blanks with words from the word box.

The principal's ________________ gave class credit for community service. Several ________________ would be available, including restoring a wetland area to its natural state and visiting the elderly in retirement homes. Students would have to spend a certain number of hours doing service to meet the ________________ requirements. The ________________, or purpose, of the community service was for the students to "learn by doing." Depending on the type of service, students would earn the ________________ of one test score in the related subject.

Day 4

Fill in the blanks with words from the word box.

When it snowed, my teacher had a great idea. He ________________ we go outside to observe the characteristics of snowflakes. One ________________ of snowflakes is that no two are ________________, or the same. Although most snowflakes are hexagons, each one is ________________. My teacher also taught us the idea of symmetry. This ________________ means that if you split a snowflake down the middle, each half would look the same. He conducted a ________________ in which he caught several snowflakes on a black piece of paper. We observed the symmetry and originality of each snowflake. It was so interesting!

Day 5

Crossword Challenge

For each clue, write one of the words from the word box to complete the puzzle.

character
conceive
conceptualize
demonstrate
exaggerate
exaggeration
minimize
narrate
narration
narrator
optional
proposal
trait

Across

1. to make something seem more important than it is
4. a suggestion or plan
9. the act of narrating
11. a special quality or feature of someone
12. to make something as small as possible

Down

1. the act of exaggerating
2. not required
3. to form a concept or idea
5. to teach by showing how to do something
6. things that make one person different from another
7. to form in the mind
8. to tell the story
10. a person who tells a story

Words for Weeks 10–17

Week 10
- infer
- inference
- surmise
- contemplate

Week 11
- involve
- exclude
- omit
- omission

Week 12
- former
- latter

Week 13
- manner
- system
- systematic

Week 14
- strategy
- strategize
- procedure
- method

Week 15
- account
- account for
- version

Week 16
- analyze
- analysis
- classify
- classification

Week 17
- acquire
- accumulate
- accumulation
- compile

infer
DAY 1

(verb) To draw a conclusion after considering specific evidence or facts.

*Students can **infer** from the materials on their desks that they are doing an experiment today.*

inference
DAY 2

(noun) A conclusion drawn by reasoning from facts and evidence.

*When Sean didn't attend the audition, we made the **inference** that he didn't want to be in the play.*

surmise
DAY 3

(verb) To draw a conclusion without certain knowledge; suppose.

*I **surmise** that we will go on vacation this year, but my parents haven't said anything yet.*

contemplate
DAY 4

(verb) To think about deeply and seriously.

*The teacher will **contemplate** the students' suggestions.*

Day 1 infer

1. How would you complete this sentence? Say it aloud to a partner.

You can infer how popular a celebrity is by ________.

2. Which word is a synonym for *infer*? Circle your answer.

a. choose
b. interrupt
c. determine
d. concentrate

3. Which sentence uses *infer* correctly? Circle your answer.

a. You can infer a character's thoughts from the character's actions.
b. To infer a character's actions, you need a magnifying glass.
c. There are too many characters to make an infer.
d. I could infer what he said to me several times.

4. How might you *infer* that someone had looked through your desk?

____

____

Day 2 inference

1. How would you complete this sentence? Say it aloud to a partner.

If a classmate is not in his or her chair, you could make the inference that ________.

2. Which of these would help you make an *inference* from a class science experiment? Circle your answer.

a. listening to other science students, even when their facts are wrong
b. reading your notes of what happened during the experiment
c. watching a science fiction movie that shows an experiment
d. taking a guess before the experiment begins

3. Which words are <u>not</u> synonyms for *inference*? Circle your answers.

a. conclusion
b. judgment
c. boredom
d. correction

4. What is an *inference* you can make about studying academic vocabulary?

____

Day 3 surmise

1. How would you complete this sentence? Say it aloud to a partner.

I surmise that I will study ________ in ________ next year.

2. In which situations would it not be a good idea to *surmise*? Circle your answer.

a. wondering what is for dinner
b. thinking about the next episode of a favorite TV show
c. choosing the correct answer to a math problem
d. taking money to the store to buy a specific book

3. Which sentence uses *surmise* correctly? Circle your answer.

a. The students surmise what the teacher told them.
b. I surmise that we will play soccer, since the soccer balls are out.
c. My birthday party was a great surmise.
d. I surmise that our next test will be difficult.

Day 4 contemplate

1. How would you complete this sentence? Say it aloud to a partner.

One important decision I contemplated was ________.

2. Which of these would you *contemplate*? Circle your answer.

a. how to help a friend
b. what to wear to school
c. what to eat for lunch
d. how to ride a bicycle

3. Which sentence does not use *contemplate* correctly? Circle your answer.

a. Veejay will contemplate long and hard before deciding on a science fair project.
b. Let's contemplate at the playground before the game.
c. The main character in the story had to contemplate before choosing a course of action.
d. Please consider all the options when you contemplate your decision.

4. What do you think your friends *contemplate*?

____

Day 5 infer • inference • surmise • contemplate

Fill in the bubble next to the correct answer.

1. Which statement is correct?

Ⓐ When you infer, you use your imagination to create ideas.
Ⓑ The best way to infer is to make a guess.
Ⓒ Good observation skills can help you infer something.
Ⓓ Knowing facts does not help you to infer.

2. In which sentence could *inference* be used to fill in the blank?

Ⓕ An ________ is a sentence that ends in a question mark.
Ⓖ You can make an ________ about the subject of a book from its title.
Ⓗ You can ________ to get an idea of how much something will cost.
Ⓙ An ________ is a picture or drawing.

3. If you *surmise* something, which of the following explains what you do?

Ⓐ think about it
Ⓑ figure it out using evidence
Ⓒ get it wrong
Ⓓ suppose

4. When you *contemplate,* which of the following do you not do?

Ⓕ be silly
Ⓖ take your time
Ⓗ consider carefully
Ⓙ think seriously

Writing If you forgot a friend's birthday, and then the friend ignored you, what could you *infer?* How did you *infer* this? Be sure to use the word *infer* in your writing.

involve
DAY 1

(verb) To have something as a necessary part; include.

*Winning the championship will **involve** beating every team.*

involve • exclude
DAY 2

involve

(verb) To bring into a situation.

*Our teacher **involves** parents as guest speakers on Occupation Day.*

---

exclude

(verb) To keep or leave something or someone out.

*We **exclude** some jobs on Occupation Day because we can't include everything.*

omit
DAY 3

(verb) To leave out; not include.

*Let's not **omit** a single event when we describe our fantastic vacation!*

omission
DAY 4

(noun) Something that is left out, removed, or not done.

*It was an **omission** to not give credit to everyone who worked on the project.*

Day 1 involve

1. **How would you complete this sentence? Say it aloud to a partner.**

   Doing well in school involves ________.

2. **If class reports *involve* doing research, what does that mean? Circle your answer.**

   a. Research is not needed for the reports.
   b. The class members are being studied for research.
   c. The reports are about people who do research.
   d. Class members need to do research for their reports.

3. **Which word is a synonym for *involve*? Circle your answer.**

   a. push
   b. require
   c. find
   d. inspire

Day 2 involve • exclude

1. **How would you complete these sentences? Say them aloud to a partner.**

   I would not want to be involved in ________.

   It is rude to exclude ________ from ________.

2. **If a friend wants to *involve* you in an activity, what does that mean? Circle your answer.**

   a. The friend wants you to be part of the activity.
   b. The friend lives far away from you.
   c. It is necessary for you to do the activity.
   d. The friend is keeping the activity a secret.

3. **Which word is a synonym for *exclude*? Circle your answer.**

   a. welcome
   b. reject
   c. excite
   d. interest

4. **If you needed help on a school project, whom would you *involve*? Why?**

____

____

Day 3 omit

1. How would you complete this sentence? Say it aloud to a partner.

If I could omit one activity from my day, it would be ________.

2. A teacher will *omit* your lowest quiz score when figuring your grade. What should that do to your grade? Circle your answer.

a. lower your grade
b. make no difference to your grade
c. raise your grade
d. cause you to fail

3. You send in a drawing to an art contest but *omit* the entry form. What did you do? Circle your answer.

a. You filled out the form incorrectly.
b. You attached the form in the wrong place.
c. You sent the form to the wrong address.
d. You did not include the entry form.

Day 4 omission

1. How would you complete this sentence? Say it aloud to a partner.

Forgetting to ________ is an omission I would never make.

2. A newspaper article about a school event included an *omission.* What happened? Circle your answer.

a. An important piece of information was not included in the article.
b. The article was very long.
c. The article included a quote from the principal.
d. The school schedule for the year was included in the article.

3. Which sentence uses *omission* correctly? Circle your answer.

a. The omission needs some ideas to make it clearer.
b. Please omission some words to make the sentence shorter.
c. One serious omission in the team list was the name of the coach.
d. If you need an omission to the report, you can add some artwork.

Day 5 involve • exclude • omit • omission

Fill in the bubble next to the correct answer.

1. Which of these does a group project not *involve*?

Ⓐ sharing ideas with others
Ⓑ team planning
Ⓒ sharing responsibilities
Ⓓ being best friends

2. In which sentence could *exclude* replace the underlined word(s)?

Ⓕ We can invite more friends to have a bigger party.
Ⓖ Everyone should try to contribute food and games.
Ⓗ The party will be better if we keep out troublemakers.
Ⓙ We need helpers to clean out the basement for the party.

3. In which sentence could the word *omit* fill in the blank?

Ⓐ We need to ________ one player because we have too many today.
Ⓑ We need to ________ one player because we have too few today.
Ⓒ We need to ________ the team to get started.
Ⓓ We need to ________ the game and continue when it stops raining.

4. Which word is an antonym for *omission*?

Ⓕ deletion
Ⓖ addition
Ⓗ opportunity
Ⓙ error

Writing What steps would be *involved* in starting a club? Explain your ideas. Be sure to use the word *involve* in your writing.

____

____

____

____

former

DAY 1

(noun) The first of two things mentioned.

*Between the first-grade teacher and the fifth-grade teacher, the **former** has been teaching longer.*

former

DAY 2

(adj.) Having to do with the past; previous.

*The **former** principal of our school returned to receive an award.*

latter

DAY 3

(noun) The second of two things mentioned.

*We will visit a museum and an aquarium, but we are more excited about the **latter** because we love fish!*

latter

DAY 4

(adj.) Near the end.

*The **latter** part of the book, after the hero is captured, is the most exciting to read.*

Day 1 former

1. How would you complete this sentence? Say it aloud to a partner.

If I have a choice to ________ or to ________, I usually choose the former.

2. You read an article that compares India and China for a report you are doing on the *former.* What is the subject of your report? Circle your answer.

a. China
b. India
c. both China and India
d. Asia

3. Which of these would help you identify the *former* of two songs sung at a concert? Circle your answer.

a. having the words to the songs in front of you
b. knowing which song your friends like
c. knowing when the concert started and finished
d. having a program that lists the order of the songs

Day 2 former

1. How would you complete this sentence? Say it aloud to a partner.

A former ________ of mine that I admire is ________.

2. A guest speaker is introduced as the city's *former* police chief. Which of these is true of the guest? Circle your answer.

a. The guest is currently the city's police chief.
b. The guest is currently the city's fire chief.
c. The guest is no longer the city's police chief.
d. The guest can no longer speak.

3. Which word is a synonym for *former*? Circle your answer.

a. past
b. friendly
c. modern
d. famous

Day 3 latter

1. How would you complete this sentence? Say it aloud to a partner.

Between fall and spring, many people prefer the latter because ________ is ________.

2. Which of these is always true of the *latter* of two choices? Circle your answer.

a. It's the best choice.
b. It's smaller than the other choice.
c. It's not the first of the choices.
d. It's the only choice.

3. At lunch you have an apple and a banana. Your friend wants the *latter* and trades an orange for it. What fruits do you have now? Circle your answer.

a. apple and banana
b. apple and orange
c. banana and orange
d. apple, banana, and orange

Day 4 latter

1. How would you complete this sentence? Say it aloud to a partner.

A holiday that falls in the latter part of the year is ________.

2. You turn on the television and find a channel playing the *latter* part of a movie you like. What does that mean? Circle your answer.

a. The movie has just ended.
b. The movie is just starting.
c. Less than half of the movie has been shown.
d. More than half of the movie has been shown.

3. Your history teacher says a quiz will cover the *latter* events in the life of a famous president. How should you prepare for the quiz? Circle your answer.

a. Review every event of his life.
b. Review the earliest events of his life.
c. Review events near the end of his life.
d. Review events that happened after he died.

4. Write about what you did in the *latter* part of your summer vacation.

____

____

Day 5 former • latter

Fill in the bubble next to the correct answer.

1. Which sentence uses *former* correctly?

Ⓐ Between winter and spring, the former is spring.
Ⓑ Every season comes former than the other.
Ⓒ Between summer and winter, the former is the hotter time of year.
Ⓓ Summer seems former every year.

2. In which sentence could *former* replace the underlined word?

Ⓕ The new school is opening this week.
Ⓖ Our previous school was built years ago.
Ⓗ The biggest school is the high school.
Ⓙ A future school may have no classrooms at all.

3. In which sentence could *latter* fill in the blank?

Ⓐ The two puppies were born in the ________ basket.
Ⓑ I was shown two puppies, Roscoe and Chloe, and I chose the ________.
Ⓒ The ________ of puppies have not been born yet.
Ⓓ One puppy was born ________ than the others.

4. Which word is an antonym for *latter*?

Ⓕ earlier
Ⓖ later
Ⓗ second
Ⓙ farther

Writing Describe one of your favorite *former* teachers or coaches. Be sure to use the word *former* in your writing.

____

____

____

____

manner

DAY 1

(noun) A way of doing things; style.

*The careful **manner** in which Harris always completes his homework impresses his teacher.*

system

DAY 2

(noun) A group of related things or parts that work together as a whole.

*The computer **system** stopped working when the electricity went off.*

system

DAY 3

(noun) A particular way or method of doing something.

*Arianna needs a better **system** for remembering her homework, because she often forgets to bring it to school.*

systematic

DAY 4

(adj.) Involving or based on a method or plan.

*A more **systematic** way to organize our class library would be to arrange the books by subject matter.*

Day 1 manner

1. How would you complete this sentence? Say it aloud to a partner.

My usual manner of greeting someone is to say ________.

2. Which word is a synonym for *manner*? Circle your answer.

a. polite
b. exhibit
c. way
d. subject

3. Your teacher announces that her *manner* of assigning homework will change. What does that mean? Circle your answer.

a. The class will no longer receive any homework.
b. The way that homework assignments are given will change.
c. The class will receive less homework.
d. How students complete their homework will need to change.

Day 2 system

1. How would you complete this sentence? Say it aloud to a partner.

Another school in our school system is ________.

2. You are studying a *system* in the human body. What are you learning? Circle your answer.

a. how specific parts of the body work together
b. how to get along better with others
c. how people look and act alike or different
d. how to improve your study skills

3. Which phrase is <u>not</u> related to the idea of a *system*? Circle your answer.

a. being connected
b. working together
c. consisting of several parts
d. working independently

4. Why is the solar *system* a *system*?

____

____

Day 3 system

1. How would you complete this sentence? Say it aloud to a partner.

Our teacher's system for checking attendance is ________.

2. In which sentence is *system* not used correctly? Circle your answer.

a. Voting is one system for choosing leaders.
b. Every library has a system for organizing materials.
c. A principal is a system for leading a school.
d. Our coach's training system helps us get in shape.

3. Which word is a synonym for *system?* Circle your answer.

a. method
b. setting
c. product
d. operation

Day 4 systematic

1. How would you complete this sentence? Say it aloud to a partner.

A systematic way to clean up my room would be to ________.

2. Which word would not describe something that is *systematic?* Circle your answer.

a. planned
b. methodical
c. careless
d. consistent

3. A school has a *systematic* approach to fire drills. What does that mean? Circle your answer.

a. The school has not planned for fire drills.
b. The school follows a specific plan for fire drills.
c. The school has evidence of a serious fire.
d. The school is down the street from the fire department.

4. Describe something you do in a *systematic* way.

____

____

____

Day 5 manner • system • systematic

Fill in the bubble next to the correct answer.

1. In which sentence could *manner* be used to fill in the blank?

Ⓐ They talked too loudly and showed terrible ________.

Ⓑ We discussed the ________ together.

Ⓒ Her ________ of working with others is to ask for their ideas.

Ⓓ We can work together to find a ________ for this problem.

2. In which sentence is *system* <u>not</u> used correctly?

Ⓕ They should work together to system their ideas.

Ⓖ There is a system of pipes for carrying water.

Ⓗ A car is an elaborate mechanical system.

Ⓙ A telephone system can connect people around the world.

3. In which sentence could *system* replace the underlined word?

Ⓐ The project <u>goal</u> is to build a working battery.

Ⓑ The main <u>problem</u> is not having enough materials.

Ⓒ The only <u>solution</u> is to change projects.

Ⓓ We need a better <u>way</u> for how we choose projects.

4. In which sentence is *systematic* used correctly?

Ⓕ Hector's teacher was systematic to his problems.

Ⓖ A systematic program will be well thought out.

Ⓗ The ideas will be connected as a systematic.

Ⓙ Olivia was systematic because she never did things the same way.

Writing Describe your *system* for doing homework. Be sure to use the word *system* in your writing.

____

____

____

____

strategy

DAY 1

(noun) A careful plan or method for achieving a goal.

*The student's **strategy** for winning the reading contest is to read a book every day.*

strategize

DAY 2

(verb) To plan or decide on a strategy.

*Our science team **strategized** on how to finish our project on time.*

procedure

DAY 3

(noun) A way of doing something following an orderly series of steps.

*The students learned the fire-safety **procedure** of stop, drop, and roll.*

method

DAY 4

(noun) A way in which something is done.

*One **method** of learning the words is to make flashcards.*

Day 1 strategy

1. **How would you complete this sentence? Say it aloud to a partner.**

   A good strategy for getting along with others at school is ________.

2. **If you learn a math *strategy* to use in solving word problems, what have you learned? Circle your answer.**

   a. why math is hard for some students
   b. some new numbers
   c. a plan for solving word problems
   d. a word problem to solve

3. **Which sentence uses *strategy* correctly? Circle your answer.**

   a. The coach has several good players to strategy.
   b. We can strategy together after the game.
   c. Our best strategy is sick today with a cold.
   d. We have a strategy for winning this game.

4. **Describe a *strategy* you could follow to read more books in a year.**

____

Day 2 strategize

1. **How would you complete this sentence? Say it aloud to a partner.**

   My friends and I sometimes strategize on how to ________.

2. **To raise money for a trip, your class needs to *strategize.* What does that mean? Circle your answer.**

   a. The class needs to give up on taking the trip.
   b. The class needs to come up with ways to raise money.
   c. The class needs to choose a place to go on a trip.
   d. The class needs to find parents who will go with them.

3. **Which of these would most likely require you to *strategize?* Circle your answer.**

   a. eating dinner
   b. sharpening your pencil
   c. completing a group project
   d. sitting at your desk

Day 3 procedure

1. How would you complete this sentence? Say it aloud to a partner.

My procedure for doing my homework is to start by ________.

2. Which word is not a synonym for *procedure*? Circle your answer.

a. confusion
b. process
c. method
d. approach

3. If you follow a *procedure* to check out books from the library, which of these is true? Circle your answer.

a. You do something different each time you check out a book.
b. There is a set of steps to follow to check out a book.
c. You can check out only one book at a time.
d. You must promise to check out books from the library.

4. Write about a new *procedure* you learned this year.

____

____

Day 4 method

1. How would you complete this sentence? Say it aloud to a partner.

The method I use for studying new words is ________.

2. Based on what you know, how would you define "scientific *method*"? Circle your answer.

a. what helps you remember how to spell "scientific"
b. how you make science
c. the way that people study and learn about science
d. doing science for a method

3. If someone tells you there are three possible *methods* for constructing a model bridge, what does that mean? Circle your answer.

a. You can construct the bridge in only one way.
b. You can build the bridge however you choose.
c. The bridge cannot be built for three reasons.
d. There are three ways you can build the bridge.

Day 5 strategy • strategize • procedure • method

Fill in the bubble next to the correct answer.

1. In which sentence could the word *strategy* fill in the blank?

Ⓐ This week we will ________ in basketball practice.
Ⓑ A reading ________ will help me comprehend better.
Ⓒ The test will be on the ________ of science.
Ⓓ A history text provides a ________ of events.

2. In which sentence could *strategize* replace the underlined words?

Ⓕ We need a <u>list of ideas</u> for a class play.
Ⓖ Our <u>purpose is</u> to include everyone in a production.
Ⓗ We <u>can include everyone</u> in making costumes and scenery.
Ⓙ We should <u>develop a plan</u> to be sure everyone has a role.

3. Which sentence does <u>not</u> describe part of a *procedure*?

Ⓐ We start the recipe by cooking some eggs and then adding milk.
Ⓑ The next step in locking up the room is to close all the windows.
Ⓒ After I go to the store, I don't know what I will be doing next.
Ⓓ The fire drill ends with all students returning to their classrooms.

4. Which word is a synonym for *method*?

Ⓕ way
Ⓖ kind
Ⓗ revision
Ⓙ retreat

Writing Describe the *procedure* that is followed during a *Daily Academic Vocabulary* lesson. Be sure to use at least one of this week's words in your writing.

____

____

____

____

account

DAY 1

(noun) A written or spoken description of something that has happened.

*Each student will give an **account** of the class field trip.*

account for

DAY 2

(verb) To explain.

*We can **account for** the missing equipment, which was loaned to another team.*

version

DAY 3

(noun) A description or account from a particular point of view.

*Each child had a different **version** of how the window was broken.*

version

DAY 4

(noun) A changed or different form of something.

*Adam chose to include a pink rose instead of a red rose in his **version** of the flower painting.*

Day 1 account

1. How would you complete this sentence? Say it aloud to a partner.

An account of my family's best vacation would include ________.

2. Your parent wants an *account* of your after-school activities. What do you need to provide? Circle your answer.

a. how much you spend on snacks
b. a teacher's signature on your homework
c. a description of what you did after school
d. evidence that you go to school

3. You are to read an *account* of a person's trip to another country. Which of these would you not expect to learn? Circle your answer.

a. details about what happened on the trip
b. what the person's life is like at home
c. information on the places that the person visited
d. how the person felt about the trip

Day 2 account for

1. How would you complete this sentence? Say it aloud to a partner.

I had to account for my whereabouts when ________.

2. Your teacher asks you to *account for* a math error you made. What do you need to do? Circle your answer.

a. do extra work to make up for a bad grade
b. correct the error you made
c. count the number of math errors you have made lately
d. explain why you think you made the error

3. Which sentence uses *account for* correctly? Circle your answer.

a. Our team needs to account for why we lost the game.
b. If we had an account for the game, we would win.
c. Let's invite the winners to account for us.
d. When there is an account for winning, everyone is happy.

4. How could you *account for* a lost pencil?

____

Day 3 version

1. How would you complete this sentence? Say it aloud to a partner.

A friend and I once gave different versions of how ________.

2. You are reading a character's *version* of an event in a story. What does that mean? Circle your answer.

a. You are getting the character's description of the event.
b. No one in the story knows about the event.
c. The story is about an event that really happened.
d. You are reading a description of the character.

3. Which phrase would <u>not</u> be used to describe two people's *versions* of an event that took place two years ago? Circle your answer.

a. similar in most respects
b. different in some details
c. completely identical
d. mostly the same

Day 4 version

1. How would you complete this sentence? Say it aloud to a partner.

I have heard different versions of the song "________."

2. Which statement explains how to make a new *version* of your favorite sandwich? Circle your answer.

a. Make the exact same sandwich you always make.
b. Make another kind of sandwich and not your favorite sandwich.
c. Don't make a sandwich at all.
d. Make your favorite sandwich but use a new kind of bread.

3. A particular movie is a *version* of a popular book. What does that mean? Circle your answer.

a. The movie is not as popular as the book.
b. The movie is based on the book but is different in some ways.
c. The movie is boring.
d. The movie is more fun to watch than reading the book.

4. Write a two-sentence *version* of a fairy tale.

____

____

Day 5 account • account for • version

Fill in the bubble next to the correct answer.

1. Which word is a synonym for *account*?

Ⓐ report
Ⓑ problem
Ⓒ pattern
Ⓓ dream

2. Which of these describes what you are doing when you *account for* your behavior?

Ⓕ trying to control your behavior
Ⓖ promising to improve your behavior
Ⓗ giving an explanation of your behavior
Ⓙ learning new behavior

3. In which sentence could *version* fill in the blank?

Ⓐ The ________ to this problem is hard to find.
Ⓑ That event would make a good ________ in a movie.
Ⓒ We can ________ the story to make it more interesting.
Ⓓ His ________ of the accident was different from mine.

4. To create a *version* of something, what do you need to do?

Ⓕ ruin it
Ⓖ change it
Ⓗ clean it
Ⓙ count it

Writing Give an *account* of a recent activity you enjoyed doing. Use at least one of this week's words in your writing.

analyze

DAY 1

(verb) To examine something in great detail in order to understand it.

*The teacher will **analyze** the test results to determine what skills students need help on.*

analysis

DAY 2

(noun) A careful study of the parts of something in order to better understand the whole.

*The principal's **analysis** of the new rules showed that they help students get along better.*

classify

DAY 3

(verb) To put things into groups based on their characteristics.

*We can **classify** our family's pets into two groups—those with fur and those with feathers.*

classification

DAY 4

(noun) An arrangement of things into groups based on their characteristics.

*One simple **classification** of books is fiction and nonfiction.*

Day 1 analyze

1. How would you complete this sentence? Say it aloud to a partner.

I would need help if I had to analyze ________.

2. Which word is not a synonym for *analyze*? Circle your answer.

a. investigate
b. evaluate
c. imitate
d. examine

3. Which of these would best help you to *analyze* why two friends are not getting along? Circle your answer.

a. talking to both friends to get their points of view
b. siding with one friend against the other
c. trying not to learn too much about why they are not getting along
d. telling the friends to shake hands and make up

4. Name something you think would be interesting to *analyze.* How could you *analyze* it?

____

Day 2 analysis

1. How would you complete this sentence? Say it aloud to a partner.

An analysis of my typical day would show that I spend a lot of time ________.

2. Which sentence uses *analysis* correctly? Circle your answer.

a. The scientist made an analysis that blew up in the lab.
b. The analysis of the story included descriptions of the main characters.
c. The teacher will analysis our grades to decide if we need more homework.
d. The country's big events will be analysis in the future.

3. A coach asks team members to do an *analysis* of a winning game. Which of these would not be part of the process? Circle your answer.

a. identifying examples of teamwork in the game
b. identifying good plays in the game
c. identifying bad plays in the game
d. identifying players for next year's team

An **analysis** of the moon will reveal its effects on the tides.

Day 3 classify

1. How would you complete this sentence? Say it aloud to a partner.

Something that people classify by size is ________.

2. Describe three ways to *classify* different kinds of sports.

a. ________________________________

b. ________________________________

c. ________________________________

3. Which of these would you not need to do to *classify* a set of objects by the sounds they make? Circle your answer.

a. listen to the objects
b. group the objects by type of sound
c. identify the objects that have similar sounds
d. choose the objects that have similar shapes

Day 4 classification

1. How would you complete this sentence? Say it aloud to a partner.

________ and ________ are two foods that fall under the classification of ________.

2. Which of these would be most helpful in the *classification* of plants? Circle your answer.

a. observing plants to identify their characteristics
b. watering them on a regular basis
c. observing different insects that live on plants
d. planting seeds to grow a garden

3. An exhibit on the *classification* of butterflies would focus on which of the following? Circle your answer.

a. how to grow a garden that attracts butterflies
b. how a caterpillar becomes a butterfly
c. butterflies' different colors, sizes, and patterns on their wings
d. why butterflies are popular insects

Day 5 analyze • analysis • classify • classification

Fill in the bubble next to the correct answer.

1. Which of these are the most important skills to use when you *analyze*?

Ⓐ teaching skills
Ⓑ thinking skills
Ⓒ cooking skills
Ⓓ art skills

2. In which sentence could *analysis* be used to fill in the blank?

Ⓕ The class is doing an experiment and then will ________ the results.
Ⓖ Keeping ________ during the experiment will help us write our report.
Ⓗ The main purpose of the experiment is to test for ________.
Ⓙ An ________ of the experiment showed a different result than the class expected.

3. Which word describes what you do when you *classify*?

Ⓐ multiply
Ⓑ copy
Ⓒ organize
Ⓓ exclaim

4. Which of these would not be used in the *classification* of animals?

Ⓕ how they move
Ⓖ what they eat
Ⓗ where they live
Ⓙ what they think about

Writing Describe a way in which you could *classify* the different books that you have read. Use at least one of this week's words in your writing.

___

___

___

___

acquire

DAY 1

(verb) To get as your own.

*I just **acquired** a new bike.*

accumulate

DAY 2

(verb) To collect, gather together, or let pile up.

*I will **accumulate** many rocks in order to build a wall.*

accumulation

DAY 3

(noun) An amount that collects or piles up.

*There is an **accumulation** of empty bottles in the garage.*

compile

DAY 4

(verb) To collect or put together in an orderly form.

*We should **compile** the list of sources that we used for our report.*

Day 1 acquire

1. How would you complete this sentence? Say it aloud to a partner.

Something I would like my family to acquire is ________.

2. Students must *acquire* a uniform for school. What does that mean? Circle your answer.

a. Every student is against uniforms.
b. Students want to dress the same.
c. Every student must get a school uniform.
d. Students will come to school in one group.

3. Which of these would help you most to *acquire* a particular skill? Circle your answer.

a. having a friend with this skill
b. learning and practicing the skill yourself
c. watching your teacher use the skill
d. hearing about what you can do with this skill

4. Name something you recently *acquired.* How did you *acquire* it?

____

Day 2 accumulate

1. How would you complete this sentence? Say it aloud to a partner.

Something that can accumulate on the ground is ________.

2. Emma spends a week at the beach and *accumulates* seashells. What does that mean? Circle your answer.

a. She throws away all the seashells she finds.
b. She buries many seashells on the beach.
c. She sells many seashells at the beach.
d. She finds and collects many seashells.

3. You need to *accumulate* information for a report. What do you need to do? Circle your answer.

a. gather information to use in the report
b. throw out information you don't need
c. collect reports
d. think of a topic for a report

Day 3 accumulation

1. How would you complete this sentence? Say it aloud to a partner.

In my room I have an accumulation of ________.

2. Which word would not be used to describe an *accumulation*? Circle your answer.

a. growing c. friendly
b. increasing d. large

3. Juana has an *accumulation* of newspaper. Which sentence best explains why she has an *accumulation*? Circle your answer.

a. She picked up her neighbor's newspaper this morning.
b. She kept every day's newspaper for a month.
c. She gave many newspapers away.
d. She asked for a job at a newspaper.

Day 4 compile

1. How would you complete this sentence? Say it aloud to a partner.

Something that a family might compile is ________.

2. Which word is a synonym for *compile*? Circle your answer.

a. sort c. assemble
b. write d. edit

3. Your teacher asks you to *compile* a list of materials needed for the science experiment. What do you need to do? Circle your answer.

a. Make labels for the equipment.
b. Write down the name of each item needed.
c. Look in the cupboard.
d. Do the experiment.

4. What questions would you *compile* before interviewing a famous artist? List three.

____

____

____

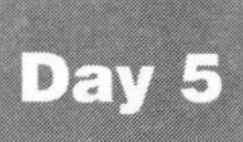

acquire • accumulate accumulation • compile

Fill in the bubble next to the correct answer.

1. Which sentence uses *acquire* correctly?

Ⓐ I have to acquire an illness for school.

Ⓑ I need to acquire a library card to check out books.

Ⓒ Hannah wants to acquire herself in a new dress.

Ⓓ There is one acquire that all students must meet.

2. In which sentence could *accumulate* fill in the blank?

Ⓕ It would be fun to ________ exhibits at the museum.

Ⓖ It would be fun to ________ stars on a summer night.

Ⓗ It would be fun to ________ rare baseball cards.

Ⓙ It would be fun to ________ a party for all of my friends.

3. Which word would not be used as a synonym for *accumulation?*

Ⓐ invitation

Ⓑ pile

Ⓒ stack

Ⓓ collection

4. Which sentence does not use *compile* correctly?

Ⓕ We can compile our stories into a book.

Ⓖ We need to compile a list of camping supplies.

Ⓗ We can go to the market to compile our dinner.

Ⓙ We have a week to compile the information.

Writing Explain a good way to *acquire* information about a subject that interests you. Be sure to use the word *acquire* in your writing.

____

____

____

____

REVIEW: Weeks 10–17

Daily Academic Vocabulary

accumulates	**classifications**	**excludes**	**latter**	**omission**
acquiring	**classified**	**former**	**manner**	**strategy**

Day 1

Fill in the blanks with words from the word box.

What do pencils and diamonds have in common? Although people write with the ____________________ and wear the ____________________, both a pencil "lead" and a diamond are made of pure carbon. Carbon, the sixth element on the periodic chart, is ____________________ as a nonmetal. It is a basic building block in over 10 million organisms and substances! In a pencil "lead," the carbon atoms group together in layers. When carbon piles up and ____________________ deep underground, the atoms group together in cubes and form diamonds. With the help of diamond's plain gray-black cousin, you can create writing that sparkles!

Day 2

Fill in the blanks with words from the word box.

We have two ____________________ for players on our volleyball team, beginning and advanced. My coach thinks I might have a chance to play with the advanced players this year if I use a ____________________ of consistent practice and effort. I'm already working on ____________________ more skills, such as a stronger serve. I am working on my ____________________ of cooperation with other players, too. My coach told me that it's often the ____________________ of team spirit and lack of effort that ____________________ players from moving up to the advanced team. I am going to work as hard as I can!

REVIEW: Weeks 10–17

Daily Academic Vocabulary

account	**analyzed**	**infer**	**omitted**	**systematic**
account for	**compiled**	**involved**	**system**	**version**

Day 3

Fill in the blanks with words from the word box.

Tracking was my favorite part of outdoor science camp. We had to use facts and observations to __________________ what kind of animal made the track. One of the ways we __________________ a track was to count the number of toes the animal had. Then we measured the length and depth of the track. Other information was gathered in a __________________ way and __________________ in lists. This included the direction the track was going and what animals lived in the area. However, sometimes factors such as rain would __________________ us not finding many tracks.

Day 4

Fill in the blanks with words from the word box.

Naomi and her younger sister, Alicia, each wrote an __________________ of their trip to Puerto Rico. Naomi described the bustling capital city, San Juan, and the island's public transportation __________________. Traveling __________________ small vans and winding roads as opposed to the buses and freeways at home. Alicia's __________________ of the trip included details about the delicious fried banana-like plantains and the diversity of marine life. She didn't want to remember the winding roads, so she __________________ that part from her description. Both girls were able to practice their Spanish and have fun!

Crack the Code!

Write one of the words from the word box on the lines next to each clue.

account	**analyze**	**former**	**method**	**strategy**
account for	**classification**	**infer**	**omission**	**surmise**
accumulate	**classify**	**inference**	**omit**	**system**
accumulation	**compile**	**involve**	**procedure**	**systematic**
acquire	**contemplate**	**latter**	**proceed**	**version**
analysis	**exclude**	**manner**	**strategize**	

1. an amount that collects __ __ __ __ __ __ __ __ __ __ __ __ (1 under letter 6, 2 under letter 7)

2. a careful study of the parts to understand the whole __ __ __ __ __ __ __ __ (3 under letter 3)

3. to think about seriously __ __ __ __ __ __ __ __ __ __ __ (4 under letter 1)

4. to suppose or guess __ __ __ __ __ __ __ (5 under letter 4)

5. an answer found by using facts you learn __ __ __ __ __ __ __ __ __ (6 under letter 5)

6. a step-by-step way of doing something __ __ __ __ __ __ __ __ __ (7 under letter 6)

7. a way in which something is done __ __ __ __ __ __ (8 under letter 3)

8. to use a strategy to plan __ __ __ __ __ __ __ __ __ __ (9 under letter 1, 10 under letter 10)

Now use the numbers under the letters to crack the code. Write the letters on the lines below. The words will complete this sentence:

Because they are so hard, diamonds are used to _______.

__ __ __   h __ __ __   __ __ __ __ __ __

4 1 8   3 6 7   5 10 8 3 2 9

Words for Weeks 19–26

Week 19
approximate
approximately
comparable
absolute
absolutely

Week 20
debate
issue

Week 21
concise
compact
condensed
condense
cohesive

Week 22
insert
insertion
delete
deletion

Week 23
foresee
anticipate
anticipation
expectation

Week 24
subsequent
precede
preceding
prior

Week 25
distinguish
discriminate
distinction

Week 26
construct
constructive
formulate
initiate
initial

approximate
DAY 1

(adj.) More or less accurate or correct.

*We only need to report the **approximate** length of the hallway.*

approximately
DAY 2

(adv.) Not exactly, but nearly.

*We have **approximately** one hour to work on the project.*

comparable
DAY 3

(adj.) Nearly the same; similar.

*Both pairs of sneakers are **comparable** in price.*

absolute • absolutely
DAY 4

absolute

(adj.) Complete; total; without limit.

*I have **absolute** confidence in my ability to do this activity.*

---

absolutely

(adv.) Completely; totally.

*I checked my work, and I am **absolutely** sure it is correct.*

Day 1 approximate

1. How would you complete this sentence? Say it aloud to a partner.

The approximate height of my ________ is ________.

2. Your parent wants to know the *approximate* cost of a school activity. What does that mean? Circle your answer.

a. Your parent wants a close amount of how much the activity costs.
b. Your parent wants to know the exact amount that the activity will cost.
c. Your parent wants an idea of why you are interested in the activity.
d. Your parent wants you to earn the money to pay for the activity.

3. What do you think is the *approximate* number of students present in class today?

____

Day 2 approximately

1. How would you complete this sentence? Say it aloud to a partner.

There are approximately ________ until my birthday.

2. A family has planned *approximately* five days for a trip. What does that mean? Circle your answer.

a. The trip must be completed in five days.
b. The family actually has about three days for a trip.
c. Some family members will stay home if the trip takes longer than five days.
d. A family has about five days for a trip but may actually have more or fewer days.

3. Which sentence does <u>not</u> use *approximately* correctly? Circle your answer.

a. The plane will arrive at approximately 8 p.m.
b. I can give you an approximately number of students.
c. This tree will take approximately two years to bear fruit.
d. The school pond is approximately 80 feet wide.

4. *Approximately* how long does it take you to complete a *Daily Academic Vocabulary* lesson?

____

____

Day 3 comparable

1. How would you complete this sentence? Say it aloud to a partner.

Two games with comparable rules are ________ and ________.

2. If you and a friend have *comparable* skills in math, which of these is true? Circle your answer.

a. Your friend is much better in math than you are.
b. You are much better in math than your friend.
c. You and your friend have about the same ability in math.
d. Your friend always tries to do math problems faster than you.

3. Which of these would not be true of two activities that are *comparable* in difficulty? Circle your answer.

a. Both activities require about the same amount of skill.
b. One activity is much easier to do than the other.
c. One activity is about as challenging as the other.
d. Neither activity is more difficult than the other.

Day 4 absolute • absolutely

1. How would you complete these sentences? Say them aloud to a partner.

If I had absolute freedom, I would ________.

I am absolutely against ________ because ________.

2. A teacher asks for your *absolute* attention. What do you need to do? Circle your answer.

a. Keep on doing what you are doing.
b. Listen with one ear while you finish what you are doing.
c. Stop what you are doing and pay full attention to the teacher.
d. Stop what you are doing and get ready to leave the classroom.

3. Which word is not a synonym for *absolutely*? Circle your answer.

a. finally
b. entirely
c. wholly
d. completely

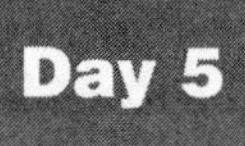

Day 5 **approximate • approximately • comparable**
absolute • absolutely

Fill in the bubble next to the correct answer.

1. In which sentence is *approximate* not used correctly?

Ⓐ Monday or Tuesday is the approximate day when the packages will arrive.

Ⓑ The approximate number of days for shipping is three or four.

Ⓒ We need an approximate number of the guests in order to buy food.

Ⓓ We will approximate the party if we know exactly when it begins.

2. Which word is an antonym for *approximately?*

Ⓕ roughly

Ⓖ precisely

Ⓗ around

Ⓙ nearly

3. If two sports are *comparable,* which statement would be used to describe them?

Ⓐ They are nothing alike.

Ⓑ The only thing they have in common is they are played by a team.

Ⓒ One sport requires helmets and the other does not.

Ⓓ Both use similar equipment and are played in much the same way.

4. In which sentence could *absolutely* replace the underlined word?

Ⓕ We will never have enough time to see the movie.

Ⓖ We can maybe have time for a visit to the beach.

Ⓗ We completely failed to send a postcard to anyone.

Ⓙ We almost ran out of water and had only one bottle left.

Writing Should anyone have *absolute* power over other people? Why or why not? Be sure to use at least one of this week's words in your writing.

debate DAY 1

(verb) To discuss the arguments for or against something.

*Our class will **debate** another class about the choice of school mascot.*

(noun) A discussion of arguments for or against something.

*There was a **debate** between two classes over the choice of school mascot.*

debate DAY 2

(verb) To think over carefully before making a decision.

*I **debated** whether to play in the band or sing in the chorus.*

issue DAY 3

(noun) A subject of debate or argument.

*The classes discussed the **issue** of student rights.*

issue DAY 4

(verb) To send or give out something.

*The principal will **issue** a statement that recognizes students for their participation in the recycling program.*

Day 1 debate

1. How would you complete these sentences? Say them aloud to a partner.

I would prepare for a debate by ________.

I would like to see a debate between ________ and ________ on the topic of ________.

2. Your teacher invites the class to *debate* the need for homework. What does that mean? Circle your answer.

a. Your teacher will no longer give homework.
b. Your class enjoys getting homework.
c. Your class will present reasons why homework is or is not helpful.
d. Your teacher will decide if homework is helpful or not for each student.

3. Which of these would not be true of a good *debate* between two classes? Circle your answer.

a. Neither class would have anything to say.
b. There would be a discussion between the classes.
c. Both sides would have different points of view.
d. Each class would present arguments to challenge the other.

Day 2 debate

1. How would you complete this sentence? Say it aloud to a partner.

Something my family might debate is ________.

2. When it starts to rain, the umpire *debates* stopping the baseball game. Which of these would not be true? Circle your answer.

a. The umpire considers the safety of both teams.
b. The umpire immediately stops the game.
c. The umpire thinks about what happens if the rain continues.
d. The umpire thinks about what happens if the game is stopped.

3. When you *debate* between two activities, what do you do? Circle your answer.

a. You find out what your friends are doing.
b. You choose the first activity you think of.
c. You flip a coin to decide.
d. You think about the positives and negatives of each activity.

Day 3 issue

1. **How would you complete this sentence? Say it aloud to a partner.**

   I think an important issue is ________.

2. **Which word would least likely be used to describe an *issue* that people argue about? Circle your answer.**

   a. unimportant
   b. critical
   c. political
   d. interesting

3. **If the *issue* for a family is where to go on vacation, what does that mean? Circle your answer.**

   a. Everyone in the family agrees on where to go for a vacation.
   b. No one in the family wants to take a vacation.
   c. The family is discussing where to go on vacation.
   d. The family is on vacation and doesn't want to leave.

Day 4 issue

1. **How would you complete this sentence? Say it aloud to a partner.**

   A weather expert might issue a warning about ________.

2. **Players *issue* a challenge to another team. What does that mean? Circle your answer.**

   a. The players are fighting on the field.
   b. The players send a challenge to another team.
   c. The players produce a magazine for the other team.
   d. The players are afraid of a challenge.

3. **When schools *issue* a schedule for the year, what do they do? Circle your answer.**

   a. They give out a schedule for when school is in session.
   b. They keep the schedule a secret.
   c. They look for someone to create a schedule.
   d. They argue about which days students will be in school.

Day 5 debate • issue

Fill in the bubble next to the correct answer.

1. Which of these would not be required to *debate* someone?

Ⓐ a topic to discuss
Ⓑ a strong opinion
Ⓒ speaking or writing your ideas
Ⓓ a very loud voice

2. In which sentence could *debate* fill in the blank?

Ⓕ My science report will include a ________ and a summary.
Ⓖ There is often a ________ among scientists over a theory.
Ⓗ The science experiment needs a ________ to be complete.
Ⓙ We can find a ________ to display for the science fair.

3. In which sentence could *debate* replace the underlined word?

Ⓐ We need to arrange a time to meet for the movie.
Ⓑ I have chores to complete before the movie.
Ⓒ I need to consider whether to ride the bus or walk.
Ⓓ We need to discover a new way to get around.

4. Which pair of words are both synonyms for *issue*?

Ⓕ subject—send
Ⓖ factor—translate
Ⓗ idea—attempt
Ⓙ process—include

Writing Describe an *issue* that friends may argue about and explain how to deal with it. Be sure to use at least one of this week's words in your writing.

concise

DAY 1

(adj.) Saying a lot in a few words.

*A dictionary gives a **concise** definition of each word.*

compact

DAY 2

(adj.) Not taking up too much space.

*We have small lockers so our belongings have to be **compact**.*

condensed • condense

DAY 3

condensed

(adj.) Shortened or made smaller.

*A **condensed** story has the less important parts cut out.*

---

condense

(verb) To make smaller or shorter.

*You must **condense** the report to fit on only one page.*

cohesive

DAY 4

(adj.) Holding or working together as a whole.

*A **cohesive** team cooperates to get a job done.*

Day 1 concise

1. How would you complete this sentence? Say it aloud to a partner.

If asked to give a concise description of our classroom, I would say ________.

2. If your teacher asks for a clear and *concise* answer, what should you do? Circle your answer.

a. Answer in the form of a short report.
b. Answer very quickly.
c. Describe the entire process you followed to get the answer.
d. Give an answer that is brief and to the point.

3. Which phrase would describe a *concise* explanation? Circle your answer.

a. careless and foolish
b. twisting and turning
c. short and direct
d. long and boring

4. Give a *concise* answer to this question: What do you learn by studying academic vocabulary?

____

____

____

Day 2 compact

1. How would you complete this sentence? Say it aloud to a partner.

Something compact that I own is ________.

2. Which word is an antonym for *compact*? Circle your answer.

a. enormous
b. miniature
c. slender
d. reduced

3. Which of these would not be true of a *compact* car? Circle your answer.

a. It has two doors.
b. It is very long and wide.
c. It can carry a few people.
d. It can fit in small parking spaces.

Day 3 condensed • condense

1. How would you complete these sentences? Say them aloud to a partner.

_________ can be condensed.

I would condense _________ by _________.

2. If you had a *condensed* week of school, what would that mean? Circle your answer.

a. You would have a tough week at school.
b. Your class would shrink in size.
c. There would be fewer days of school than normal.
d. There would be fewer students at school than normal.

3. Which sentence uses *condense* corrrectly? Circle your answer.

a. If we condense the map, it will be larger and easier to read.
b. Everything is wet because of the condense outside.
c. My friends and I can condense for a short time.
d. We could condense our trip if we eliminate a few stops.

How can I **condense** this book?

BIG BIRD BOOK

Day 4 cohesive

1. How would you complete this sentence? Say it aloud to a partner.

A cohesive family would _________.

2. Which word is a synonym for *cohesive?* Circle your answer.

a. disorganized
b. united
c. disloyal
d. precise

3. Which of these does not describe a *cohesive* plan of action? Circle your answer.

a. It does not make any sense.
b. It is clear how the steps lead to a final product.
c. Each step of the plan leads to the next step.
d. It holds together and shows good thinking.

4. How would you describe a *cohesive* piece of writing?

____

____

Day 5 **concise • compact • condensed condense • cohesive**

Fill in the bubble next to the correct answer.

1. In which sentence is *concise* used correctly?

Ⓐ Her letters are concise and filled with news about people we don't even know.
Ⓑ The concise man was big and tall, just like the tall tales he liked to tell.
Ⓒ We need concise directions so we are not confused by too much information.
Ⓓ The concise description of the house included every little detail.

2. In which sentence is *compact* <u>not</u> used correctly?

Ⓕ The backpack is compact and easy to carry.
Ⓖ Bunk beds are compact and good for a small room.
Ⓗ A compact computer can fit in almost any work area.
Ⓙ A compact notebook is larger than the usual kind.

3. In which sentence could *condensed* replace the underlined word?

Ⓐ This activity is <u>shorter</u> and takes less time than the original.
Ⓑ There is a <u>larger</u> part of the puzzle to finish.
Ⓒ There is a <u>surprise</u> ending to that story.
Ⓓ This photograph is <u>brighter</u> than the others.

4. In which sentence could *condense* fill in the blank?

Ⓕ The movie had to ________ new characters to make the story more interesting.
Ⓖ The poem is long, but we will ruin the rhyming pattern if we ________ it.
Ⓗ The play is better when we ________ characters that are not needed.
Ⓙ The novel is about the main character trying to ________ his family.

Writing Describe your idea of a *cohesive* group of friends. Be sure to use the word *cohesive* in your writing.

____

____

____

____

insert • insertion DAY 1

insert

(verb) To put or place inside something. — *You should **insert** a comma between the city and state.*

insertion

(noun) The act of inserting. — *The **insertion** of a comma will correct the error.*

insertion DAY 2

(noun) Something, such as a word or phrase, that has been inserted. — *A comma was the only **insertion** that was needed in your entire report.*

delete • deletion DAY 3

delete

(verb) To remove from a piece of writing or computer text. — *Please **delete** the period and add a question mark.*

deletion

(noun) The act of deleting. — *The **deletion** of a period takes one touch of a computer key.*

deletion DAY 4

(noun) Something, such as a word or phrase, that has been deleted. — *You made the wrong **deletion** and now the sentence doesn't make sense.*

Day 1 insert • insertion

1. How would you complete these sentences? Say them aloud to a partner.

I would like to insert ________ into my usual day.

The insertion of more books on the classroom shelves would ________.

2. During a science experiment, you *insert* a straw into a bottle. What do you do? Circle your answer.

a. Use the straw to drink.
b. Place the straw next to the bottle.
c. Put the straw inside the bottle.
d. Measure the straw and the bottle.

3. Which sentence uses *insertion* correctly? Circle your answer.

a. The insertion of an extra hour makes our school day longer.
b. More students would take part in an art class insertion.
c. The coaches plan to insertion a new sport this year.
d. The student has an insertion of the rules to explain.

Day 2 insertion

1. How would you complete this sentence? Say it aloud to a partner.

When I check my writing, I often have to make an insertion of ________.

2. An *insertion* is needed to correct a misspelled word. What does that mean? Circle your answer.

a. You have used the wrong letter.
b. You need to add the missing letter.
c. You need to write a new sentence.
d. A sentence is missing many important words.

3. Which of these would never be true of a sentence after an *insertion* was added? Circle your answer.

a. The sentence would be clearer.
b. The sentence would be longer.
c. The sentence would be more interesting.
d. The sentence would be shorter.

Day 3 delete • deletion

1. How would you complete these sentences? Say them aloud to a partner.

I would like to delete ________ from my usual week.

I think the deletion of ________ from ________ would be a good idea.

2. The cafeteria has to *delete* items from the lunch menu. What does that mean? Circle your answer.

a. There will be fewer items on the menu.
b. There will be more items on the menu.
c. The menu will not change.
d. The cafeteria will stop serving lunch.

3. The *deletion* of a rule would have what result? Circle your answer.

a. The wording of the rule would change.
b. The rule would no longer have to be followed.
c. The rule would be easier to understand.
d. The rule would only be used now and then.

Day 4 deletion

1. How would you complete this sentence? Say it aloud to a partner.

The deletion of ________ would make a paragraph hard to read.

2. Which word is an antonym for *deletion?* Circle your answer.

a. improvement
b. direction
c. illustration
d. addition

3. Which sentence uses *deletion* correctly? Circle your answer.

a. The deletion made the sentence too wordy.
b. One more deletion will add just the right word.
c. This deletion made the sentence more concise.
d. A sentence that needs a deletion is usually too clear.

4. Rewrite this sentence, but with a *deletion:*
If at first you don't succeed, try, try again.

____

____

Day 5 insert • insertion • delete • deletion

Fill in the bubble next to the correct answer.

1. Which of these would not be an example of an *insertion*?

Ⓐ a word in a sentence
Ⓑ a sentence in a paragraph
Ⓒ a paragraph in an essay
Ⓓ a title of a story

2. In which sentence does *insertion* mean "the act of inserting"?

Ⓕ The insertion of a heavy object caused the tub of water to overflow.
Ⓖ That block in the middle was the insertion that made the tower stronger.
Ⓗ That phrase was a great insertion to add to our conclusion.
Ⓙ Adding his opinion was the wrong insertion when facts were needed.

3. When you delete something, what happens to the *deletion*?

Ⓐ It is added.
Ⓑ It is gone.
Ⓒ It is revised.
Ⓓ It is not changed.

4. In which sentence could *deletion* fill in the blank?

Ⓕ The ________ of the cooking class means no more cooking lessons.
Ⓖ The ________ of our team means we will get to play ball this year.
Ⓗ The ________ of that mystery will continue for a long time.
Ⓙ The ________ of a new planet would be an exciting adventure.

Writing Describe a rule that you would *insert* into a set of rules for your team, class, or school. Use the word *insert* or *insertion* in your writing.

____

____

____

____

foresee
DAY 1

(verb) To see or realize in advance that something will happen.

*The teacher could **foresee** that the students who followed the directions carefully would produce a better project.*

anticipate • anticipation
DAY 2

anticipate

(verb) To expect.

*The students **anticipate** the usual Friday quiz.*

---

anticipation

(noun) The act or process of anticipating.

*In **anticipation** of the Friday quiz, most students reviewed their notes on Thursday.*

expectation
DAY 3

(noun) The feeling or belief that something is likely to happen.

*It is our **expectation** that we will have fun on the field trip.*

expectation
DAY 4

(noun) A standard of conduct or performance expected.

*The student lived up to the **expectations** of her teacher by passing the test.*

Day 1 foresee

1. How would you complete this sentence? Say it aloud to a partner.

I can foresee that I will ________ if I ________.

2. A baseball heads for a window and you *foresee* the window breaking. What does that mean? Circle your answer.

a. You plan to break the window.
b. You know the window will break before it happens.
c. You wish the window would break.
d. You saw a broken window and guessed what happened.

3. The music teacher says she can *foresee* a career for you as a singer. What does that mean? Circle your answer.

a. She has excellent sight.
b. She believes in working hard to be a good singer.
c. She likes to listen to you sing.
d. She believes you could work as a singer someday.

Day 2 anticipate • anticipation

1. How would you complete these sentences? Say them aloud to a partner.

I anticipate that I will ________ this year because ________.

In my family, the anticipation before ________ is always exciting because ________.

2. If you *anticipate* that you will get a high score on a test, which of these is not true? Circle your answer.

a. You expect to do well on the test.
b. You will be surprised if you get a bad grade.
c. You will be shocked if you get a good grade.
d. You knew the information on the test.

3. The *anticipation* of a game makes the team nervous. What does that mean? Circle your answer.

a. The game was played and the team lost.
b. The team is nervous from thinking about the game.
c. The team is nervous because no one knows where the game will be played.
d. No one expects the team to win.

Day 3 expectation

1. How would you complete this sentence? Say it aloud to a partner.

An expectation I have for next week is that ________ will happen because ________.

2. People have the *expectation* that the storm could cause a flood. What does that mean? Circle your answer.

a. People are hoping for rain.
b. People are predicting a flood could occur.
c. People have just learned that storms cause floods.
d. People talk too much about the weather.

3. If your *expectation* is that science classes will be more difficult in college, then which of these is true? Circle your answer.

a. You believe that science classes will be harder in college.
b. You hope that science class is more work in college.
c. You know that science classes will be easier in college.
d. You think science is fun to learn.

Day 4 expectation

1. How would you complete this sentence? Say it aloud to a partner.

I hope to live up to the expectations of ________.

2. Which of these is least likely to be your *expectation* of a movie with your favorite star? Circle your answer.

a. You think it will be fun to see the movie.
b. You think you will enjoy the movie.
c. You think the star will do a good job.
d. You think the movie will be terrible.

3. The coach's *expectation* of the team is high. What does that mean? Circle your answer.

a. The coach is looking up at the team.
b. The coach has a team of tall players.
c. The coach expects the team to do well.
d. The coach wonders if the team can win.

4. What is an *expectation* you have of your friends?

____

Day 5 foresee • anticipate anticipation • expectation

Fill in the bubble next to the correct answer.

1. What can you do if you are able to *foresee* a problem?

Ⓐ Solve the problem after it occurs.

Ⓑ Let the problem get bigger.

Ⓒ Avoid the problem before it occurs.

Ⓓ Make a mistake.

2. Which word or phrase is a synonym for *anticipate*?

Ⓕ expect

Ⓖ move ahead

Ⓗ give up

Ⓙ give back

3. In which sentence could *anticipation* fill in the blank?

Ⓐ My ________ was not fun because it rained.

Ⓑ I look forward to summer with happy ________.

Ⓒ The ________ was noisy because of so many people.

Ⓓ We plan to have lots of ________ this summer.

4. Which word is not a synonym for *expectation*?

Ⓕ belief

Ⓖ prediction

Ⓗ assumption

Ⓙ accomplishment

Writing Who has *expectations* for you? What are they? Do you think you will fulfill those *expectations?* Use at least one of this week's words in your writing.

subsequent
DAY 1

(adj.) Coming after in time or order.

*If we lose this round, we will need to win the **subsequent** round to stay in the tournament.*

precede
DAY 2

(verb) To come before in time.

*For many children, a year of preschool **precedes** kindergarten.*

preceding
DAY 3

(adj.) Coming just before.

*The sky grew very dark in the moments **preceding** the storm.*

prior
DAY 4

(adj.) Earlier in time or coming before.

*We build on **prior** knowledge to learn something new.*

Day 1 subsequent

1. **How would you complete this sentence? Say it aloud to a partner.**

   In subsequent years, I expect to ________.

2. **Your teacher announces that *subsequent* classes will be held in the library. What does that mean? Circle your answer.**
   a. Small classes will meet in the library.
   b. Classes with a substitute teacher will go to the library.
   c. The next classes will be held in the library.
   d. The lower grades are using the library.

3. **Your introductory paragraph to an essay is strong, but the *subsequent* paragraphs need work. What should you do? Circle your answer.**
   a. Revise your introductory paragraph.
   b. Focus on improving the paragraphs after the introduction.
   c. Rewrite your entire essay.
   d. Focus on improving your concluding paragraph.

Day 2 precede

1. **How would you complete this sentence? Say it aloud to a partner.**

   ________ precedes ________ in my school schedule.

2. **If a pizza party will *precede* a movie, which of these is true? Circle your answer.**
   a. Most kids will be hungry during the movie.
   b. The party will take place after the movie.
   c. Kids will have pizza during the movie.
   d. Kids will have pizza before the movie.

3. **A talk with an artist will *precede* a class tour of the art museum. What does that mean? Circle your answer.**
   a. The first activity at the museum is meeting the artist.
   b. The second activity at the museum is meeting the artist.
   c. The tour will take place first.
   d. The artist will talk during the tour.

Day 3 preceding

1. How would you complete this sentence? Say it aloud to a partner.

In the days preceding an important test, I ________.

2. Which of these is true of a bell *preceding* a fire drill? Circle your answer.

a. The bell signals that a fire drill will follow.
b. The bell rings several hours before the fire drill.
c. The bell signals that the fire drill is over.
d. There is no warning before the fire drill.

3. Which of these is always true of a *preceding* event? Circle your answer.

a. It is too long.
b. It is too short.
c. It comes before something else.
d. It comes after something else.

Day 4 prior

1. How would you complete this sentence? Say it aloud to a partner.

A sport or other activity I did prior to this year is ________.

2. If you have *prior* plans, why will you miss the game at school? Circle your answer.

a. You don't know who planned the game.
b. You don't know where the game is.
c. You would rather see your friends after the game.
d. You have other plans that you made earlier.

3. Which of these describes a *prior* solution? Circle your answer.

a. one that was just discovered
b. one that was discovered earlier
c. one that has not been discovered
d. one that does not work

4. What did you do *prior* to working on *Daily Academic Vocabulary*?

____

____

____

Daily Academic Vocabulary

Day 5 subsequent • precede • preceding • prior

Fill in the bubble next to the correct answer.

1. In which sentence is *subsequent* used correctly?

Ⓐ The subsequent information always comes first.
Ⓑ There is a subsequent to plan.
Ⓒ We can subsequent for the team that is late.
Ⓓ Each subsequent grade in school is more challenging.

2. Which word is an antonym for *precede?*

Ⓕ guide
Ⓖ follow
Ⓗ finish
Ⓙ lead

3. If the *preceding* day was a great one for you, which sentence is true?

Ⓐ Yesterday was a great day for you.
Ⓑ Last week had several great days.
Ⓒ Tomorrow will be a great day.
Ⓓ Today is a great day.

4. If you use *prior* knowledge to answer a question, which of these is true?

Ⓕ You use something you just learned to answer the question.
Ⓖ You answer the question in complete sentences.
Ⓗ You use something you already knew to answer the question.
Ⓙ You answer this question before another one.

Writing Describe a *prior* experience that has helped you this year. Be sure to use the word *prior* in your writing.

distinguish

DAY 1

(verb) To tell apart by knowing or seeing the difference between two things.

*We **distinguish** between the two students by their hair color.*

distinguish

DAY 2

(verb) To see or hear clearly.

*I could not **distinguish** her voice on the phone because she was whispering.*

discriminate

DAY 3

(verb) To see a clear difference between things, people, or behavior.

*A chef can **discriminate** between the flavors in foods.*

distinction

DAY 4

(noun) A feature that makes someone or something different.

*Even though they are twins, there are definite **distinctions** in their personalities.*

Day 1 distinguish

1. How would you complete this sentence? Say it aloud to a partner.

Two animals that are easy to distinguish between are ________ and ________.

2. Which of these would not help you to *distinguish* between two sounds? Circle your answer.

a. good eyesight
b. good hearing
c. knowing what each sound is like
d. knowing what is different about the sounds

3. If you can *distinguish* between two red flowers, which of these is true? Circle your answer.

a. The two flowers look exactly alike.
b. They have qualities that make them different.
c. Their color is the only important quality you know.
d. You cannot recognize either kind of flower.

4. What *distinguishes* you from your favorite actor?

____

____

Day 2 distinguish

1. How would you complete this sentence? Say it aloud to a partner.

Even from far away, I can usually distinguish ________ because ________.

2. A foggy day makes it hard to *distinguish* many things. What does that mean? Circle your answer.

a. You cannot smell anything.
b. You cannot see well.
c. You cannot think clearly.
d. You do not feel well.

3. You are waiting in line at a store when you *distinguish* the voice of a friend. What does that mean? Circle your answer.

a. You are thinking about shopping.
b. You are thinking about your friend, who has an unusual voice.
c. You hear the voice of your friend, who is also at the store.
d. You are bored and wish you had a friend with you.

Day 3 discriminate

1. How would you complete this sentence? Say it aloud to a partner.

When people discriminate between soccer and football, they usually think about ________.

2. To *discriminate* one character from another in a story, what must you do? Circle your answer.

a. Figure out how the characters are alike.
b. Decide which character you like best.
c. Explain what is wrong with the characters.
d. Figure out how the characters are different.

3. You cannot *discriminate* the difference between two pairs of jeans. What does that mean? Circle your answer.

a. You like one pair of jeans better than the other.
b. You think the jeans are basically alike.
c. You know that one pair of jeans belongs to you.
d. You do not know if the jeans are your size.

Day 4 distinction

1. How would you complete this sentence? Say it aloud to a partner.

A distinction between me and my best friend is ________.

2. How would you decide what gives an animal its *distinction*? Circle your answer.

a. look for qualities that make it friendly
b. look for qualities that people like
c. look for qualities that make it special
d. look for qualities that make it ordinary

3. Which sentence uses *distinction* correctly? Circle your answer.

a. Their distinction is that they act just alike.
b. Some people think an asteroid caused the distinction of dinosaurs.
c. One distinction between children and adults is size.
d. The teacher was unable to distinction between the twins.

4. What is your primary *distinction*? What makes you different from others?

____

Day 5 distinguish • discriminate • distinction

Fill in the bubble next to the correct answer.

1. If you cannot *distinguish* between twins named Mary and Carrie, which of these is true?

Ⓐ Mary and Carrie look different.
Ⓑ You always know when you see Mary.
Ⓒ You always recognize Carrie.
Ⓓ You cannot tell Mary from Carrie.

2. In which sentence could *distinguish* fill in the blank?

Ⓕ There is a fire that we need to ________.
Ⓖ We could ________ our house in the aerial photograph.
Ⓗ He will ________ how to take good photographs of the children.
Ⓙ I hope we can ________ some fun today.

Can you **distinguish** an Amazon parrot from an African Gray parrot?

3. In which sentence is *discriminate* used correctly?

Ⓐ We need to discriminate a plan.
Ⓑ If we discriminate, we should get there on time.
Ⓒ We can always see better when we discriminate.
Ⓓ We can discriminate between good and bad manners.

4. Which adjective would express the meaning of *distinction*?

Ⓕ difference
Ⓖ funny
Ⓗ average
Ⓙ general

Writing Describe a *distinction* that you like about your school or community. Be sure to use the word *distinction* in your writing.

____

____

____

____

construct

DAY 1

(verb) To build or put together.

*We **constructed** a model of the solar system from styrofoam and hangers.*

constructive

DAY 2

(adj.) Serving a useful purpose; helpful.

*His **constructive** comment helped me find a solution to my problem.*

formulate

DAY 3

(verb) To work out an idea or opinion or to state something carefully and precisely.

*We will **formulate** a persuasive plan to get permission for a field trip.*

initiate • initial

DAY 4

initiate

(verb) To start; to cause to begin.

*The warring countries will **initiate** peace talks.*

---

initial

(adj.) First, or at the beginning.

*Our **initial** plan was to see a movie, but we went hiking instead.*

Day 1 construct

1. How would you complete this sentence? Say it aloud to a partner.

To construct a ________, I need ________.

2. Your teacher asks you to *construct* a sentence. What do you need to do? Circle your answer.

a. Find a correct sentence.
b. Identify what is wrong with a sentence.
c. Use blocks with letters to build some words.
d. Put words together to form a sentence.

3. Your assignment is to *construct* a piece of artwork. Which product would not fit the assignment? Circle your answer.

a. an object you build with pieces of wood
b. a picture you make by gluing together scraps of paper
c. a picture of a painting that you cut out from a magazine
d. an object you form by gluing together tubes of cardboard

Day 2 constructive

1. How would you complete this sentence? Say it aloud to a partner.

When solving a math problem, a constructive tool is ________.

2. Which word is an antonym for *constructive?* Circle your answer.

a. purposeful
b. destructive
c. positive
d. promising

3. If a friend offers you *constructive* ideas to solve a problem, which of these is most likely to be true? Circle your answer.

a. Your friend's ideas will help you build something.
b. Your friend's ideas are not helpful.
c. Your friend's ideas may help you solve your problem.
d. Your friend's ideas will cause a problem you have to solve.

4. If a friend is having a difficult time with an assignment, what might you do that would be *constructive?*

____

____

Day 3 formulate

1. **How would you complete this sentence? Say it aloud to a partner.**

   I should formulate a plan to ________.

2. **Your science teacher challenges you to *formulate* a new invention. What do you need to do? Circle your answer.**

   a. Create a math formula for an invention.
   b. Test a new invention.
   c. Do a report on a new invention you have heard about.
   d. Develop a plan for a new invention.

3. **Which word does not describe how to work when you *formulate* something? Circle your answer.**

   a. slowly
   b. carelessly
   c. precisely
   d. thoroughly

Day 4 initiate • initial

1. **How would you complete these sentences? Say them aloud to a partner.**

   I wish my teacher would initiate ________.

   My initial impression of our class was ________.

2. **The librarian plans to *initiate* a reading contest. What does that mean? Circle your answer.**

   a. The librarian will start a reading contest.
   b. The librarian will conclude a reading contest.
   c. The librarian will judge a reading contest.
   d. The librarian will stop a reading contest.

3. **If your *initial* answer on a test was wrong, which of these would be true? Circle your answer.**

   a. You answered correctly the first time.
   b. You did not answer the question.
   c. You tried to change your second answer.
   d. You started with the wrong answer.

4. **What were your *initial* thoughts of *Daily Academic Vocabulary*? How have they changed?**

   ____

   ____

Fill in the bubble next to the correct answer.

1. In which sentence could *construct* replace the underlined word or words?

Ⓐ The community will tear down the old school.

Ⓑ The children will decorate their bedroom.

Ⓒ The family will build a doghouse in the yard.

Ⓓ The sanitation department will place a trash can on the corner.

2. In which sentence is *formulate* used correctly?

Ⓕ We learned that formulate last year.

Ⓖ It will take time to formulate an entry for the writing contest.

Ⓗ The formulate for winning a contest is to read the rules carefully.

Ⓙ All we need to formulate is a hammer and some nails.

3. In which sentence is *initiate* not used correctly?

Ⓐ Let's initiate the project today so we can finish tomorrow.

Ⓑ Let's initiate the project that was finished yesterday.

Ⓒ We can initiate the project when we get the materials.

Ⓓ They will initiate their project at the same time.

4. In which sentence can *initial* fill in the blank?

Ⓕ My ________ are the same as yours.

Ⓖ The ________ season of the year is summer.

Ⓗ Saturday is the ________ last day of every week.

Ⓙ Breakfast is the ________ meal of the day for many people.

Writing Describe a *constructive* way to work out a problem between friends. Use the word *constructive* in your writing.

REVIEW: Weeks 19–26

approximately	compact	concise	distinguish	initiated
cohesive	comparable	distinction	formulated	preceding

Day 1

Fill in the blanks with words from the word box.

Papua New Guinea is a rugged and tropical country in Oceania. Not a large country, it's ____________________ in size to the state of California. ____________________ its independence in 1975, it was a colony of Australia. A country known for its cultural diversity, a primary ____________________ is the number of languages spoken there. There are ____________________ 800 languages spoken in Papua New Guinea! It's amazing that there are so many languages in such a small and ____________________ country!

Day 2

Fill in the blanks with words from the word box.

People ____________________ President Abraham Lincoln from other historical figures not only because he ended slavery, but also because of his public speaking skills. His "Gettysburg Address" is famous for its ____________________, yet powerful, wording. This two-minute speech was ____________________ to encourage the people of the United States to work together. At the time, the Civil War was being fought and Americans were not a ____________________ people. The speech ____________________ a new way of thinking about freedom and similarities between all people, no matter what side of the war they were on.

REVIEW: Weeks 19–26

absolute	condense	debates	foresee	inserted	prior
anticipation	construct	delete	initial	issues	

Day 3

Fill in the blanks with words from the word box.

For Earth Day this year, Ms. Jorgenson's class had a series of ____________________ on environmental subjects. ____________________ to the debates, teams were assigned topics. One of the ____________________ was whether it was better to ask for paper or plastic bags at the grocery store. Teams had a week to do research and ____________________ their arguments. Many teams argued that more resources are used in making paper bags. However, paper is more recyclable than plastic, so there is no ____________________ answer. One team ultimately argued that a reusable cloth bag was the best choice.

Day 4

Fill in the blanks with words from the word box.

Warren could ____________________ that the Web site was going to be a huge success. He and a couple of friends had volunteered to ____________________, or shorten, all of the information about the ski club and post it on the Internet. So far the Web site had been a lot of hard work. In the ____________________ design, they ran out of space for graphics. They had to ____________________ some of the text. Now the graphics were ____________________ and the Web site was finished. The rest of the ski club had been waiting in ____________________. They gave the Web site designers a big round of applause.

REVIEW: Weeks 19–26

Day 5

Crossword Challenge

For each clue, write one of the words from the word box to complete the puzzle.

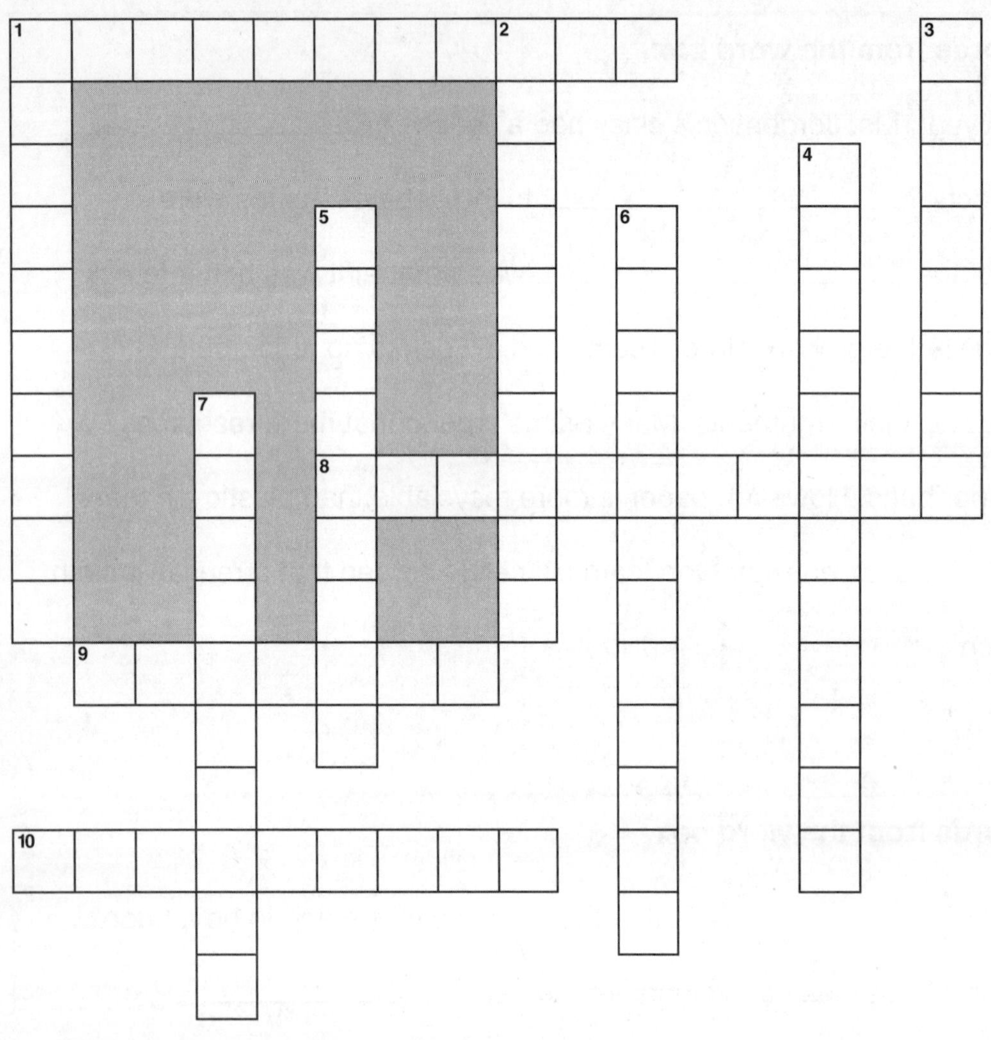

- absolutely
- anticipate
- approximate
- condensed
- constructive
- deletion
- discriminate
- expectation
- insertion
- precede
- subsequent

Across

1. more or less correct or accurate
8. the belief that something will happen
9. to come before in time
10. an object or item that has been placed between two things

Down

1. to expect
2. completely
3. something that has been removed
4. to see a clear difference between things
5. shortened or made smaller
6. serving a useful purpose
7. coming next in time or order

Words for Weeks 28–35

Week 28

integrate
integration
integral
inherent

Week 29

objective
subjective
bias
biased

Week 30

speculate
speculation
hypothesize
hypothesis
theory

Week 31

occasional
occasionally
intermittent
continuous
persistent

Week 32

probable
plausible
feasible
potential

Week 33

cite
citation
assert
validate

Week 34

explicit
implicit
denotation
connotation

Week 35

relevant
irrelevant
appropriate
pertain
pertinent

integrate
DAY 1

(verb) To combine things and make into a whole.

*I will **integrate** many subplots into my story.*

integration
DAY 2

(noun) The act of combining all parts into a whole.

*The **integration** of their group into ours will create one very strong team.*

integral
DAY 3

(adj.) Forming an essential part of something.

*Teamwork is an **integral** part of any group project.*

inherent
DAY 4

(adj.) Being a core or inborn characteristic of something.

*The student's **inherent** loyalty made him a good friend.*

Day 1 integrate

1. **How would you complete this sentence? Say it aloud to a partner.**

   I would like to integrate ________ into my daily or weekly schedule.

2. **The choir and band directors will *integrate* their ideas for the joint concert. What does that mean? Circle your answer.**

   a. The choir will have a concert instead of the band.
   b. The band will have a concert instead of the choir.
   c. The directors will combine their ideas into one concert.
   d. The directors will compete to see who has the best ideas.

3. **If a school decided to *integrate* the boys' and girls' soccer teams, which of these would be true? Circle your answer.**

   a. Some students would not be allowed to play.
   b. There would not be enough coaches for everyone.
   c. Both girls and boys would play separately.
   d. Boys and girls would play on the same team.

4. **How did your former teachers *integrate* learning with play?**

   ____

   ____

Day 2 integration

1. **How would you complete this sentence? Say it aloud to a partner.**

   The integration of various forms of technology into the classroom provides ________.

2. **A newspaper reports on the successful *integration* of a small school into a larger school. What does that mean? Circle your answer.**

   a. A small school was opened.
   b. A larger school got smaller.
   c. A small school became part of a larger school.
   d. Two schools were identified as the best for students.

3. **Which word is an antonym for *integration*? Circle your answer.**

   a. connection
   b. separation
   c. prediction
   d. rotation

Day 3 integral

1. How would you complete this sentence? Say it aloud to a partner.

________ is an integral part of school for me because ________.

2. Which word would describe an *integral* subject in school? Circle your answer.

a. essential
b. optional
c. unnecessary
d. extra

3. In health class, you learn about habits that are *integral* to good health. What does that mean? Circle your answer.

a. You learn about habits that you need to break.
b. You learn not to worry about your health.
c. You learn about how to have a good health class.
d. You learn about critical habits to follow.

Day 4 inherent

1. How would you complete this sentence? Say it aloud to a partner.

I think that an inherent quality I have is ________.

2. If investigation is *inherent* in learning science, which of these is true? Circle your answer.

a. Science knowledge is not something you can learn.
b. Investigations are an essential part of learning science.
c. Scientists don't care about investigations.
d. Science learning requires facts but not investigations.

3. Which sentence does not use *inherent* correctly? Circle your answer.

a. Freedom is inherent in a democratic society.
b. Infants have the inherent ability to learn how to walk.
c. Physical risks are inherent in many sports.
d. Humor is inherent in all books.

4. What are *inherent* qualities of a good leader?

____

____

Day 5 integrate • integration • integral • inherent

Fill in the bubble next to the correct answer.

1. In which sentence could *integrate* fill in the blank?

Ⓐ We will ________ our activities into a family fitness plan.

Ⓑ Their family plans to ________ a vacation this summer.

Ⓒ One child will ________ swimming on the lake.

Ⓓ Another child wants to ________ how to water-ski.

2. In which sentence is *integration* used correctly?

Ⓕ The zoo animals are being fed with integration.

Ⓖ The zoo staff requires integration to be safe around the animals.

Ⓗ The integration of some animals means fewer separate cages.

Ⓙ The cages at the zoo were once a symbol of integration.

3. Which word is a synonym for *integral*?

Ⓐ persuasive

Ⓑ necessary

Ⓒ temporary

Ⓓ minor

Good looks are **inherent** in parrots!

4. In which sentence is *inherent* not used correctly?

Ⓕ She has an inherent friendliness.

Ⓖ Competition is an inherent part of sports activities.

Ⓗ Many of the band members have inherent talent in music.

Ⓙ There is an inherent that links good friends.

Writing Describe an attitude or behavior that is *integral* to success in school. Be sure to use the word *integral* in your writing.

objective

DAY 1

(adj.) Based on fact, not feelings or opinions.

*The judges were **objective** and chose the winner based on the quality of the entry.*

subjective

DAY 2

(adj.) Based on feelings or opinions rather than on fact.

*The judges were **subjective** and only looked at the entries they liked.*

bias

DAY 3

(noun) A strong feeling for or against something that does not let someone be fair.

*The contest shows a **bias** for students who have talent in music or art.*

biased

DAY 4

(adj.) Favoring or opposing one person, group, or point of view more than others.

*The students were **biased** and believed their team was the best.*

Day 1 objective

1. How would you complete this sentence? Say it aloud to a partner.

It is hard to be objective when ________.

2. Which word would not describe an *objective* decision? Circle your answer.

a. fair
b. angry
c. neutral
d. careful

3. A newspaper reports on a problem in your community. What would be included in an *objective* article? Circle your answer.

a. a one-sided look at the problem
b. an emotional description of the problem
c. facts about the problem and different views of it
d. how the newspaper can solve the problem

4. In what situations do you find it hard to be *objective*? Why?

____

____

Day 2 subjective

1. How would you complete this sentence? Say it aloud to a partner.

I have a subjective opinion on ________.

2. Which of these would be true of a *subjective* history of a country? Circle your answer.

a. It would be an accurate view of events.
b. It would be a history told with just the facts.
c. It would not contain anyone's opinion of events.
d. It would be written from the author's point of view.

3. Your teacher says that a report you wrote is too *subjective*. What does that mean? Circle your answer.

a. Your report is on a very interesting subject.
b. Your penmanship looks like you were scribbling.
c. You used too many facts and made your report dull.
d. You expressed too many opinions and feelings in your report.

Day 3 bias

1. How would you complete this sentence? Say it aloud to a partner.

I have a bias for ________; I have a bias against ________.

2. Which of these would not be true of people who have a *bias* toward rock music? Circle your answer.

a. They think rock music is about the same as other kinds.
b. They like rock music more than other kinds.
c. They pay attention to rock musicians more than other kinds.
d. They go to more rock concerts than other kinds.

3. Your teacher asks you to look for *bias* in an article. What should you do? Circle your answer.

a. Try to read faster.
b. Check to see if the author is for or against someone or something.
c. Check to see if the author of the article uses humor.
d. Look for articles on the same subject to use for research.

Day 4 biased

1. How would you complete this sentence? Say it aloud to a partner.

I am biased against ________ because ________.

2. If a family is *biased* against beach vacations, which of these would be true? Circle your answer.

a. The family has always had a great time on beach vacations.
b. The family likes to go on vacations to the mountains.
c. The family dislikes beach vacations for various reasons.
d. The family does not like to go on any kind of vacation.

3. Which phrases would mean the opposite of *biased*? Circle your answers.

a. open-minded
b. come and go
c. give and take
d. middle of the road

4. Should newspapers be *biased*? Why or why not?

____

____

____

Day 5 objective • subjective • bias • biased

Fill in the bubble next to the correct answer.

1. In which sentence is *objective* used correctly?

Ⓐ They objective everything we suggest.
Ⓑ They are objective and look at both sides of the issue.
Ⓒ They are objective and spend more time with one friend than the other.
Ⓓ They are not objective and will always be late.

2. In which sentence could *subjective* fill in the blank?

Ⓕ I know I am ________, but I like our plan better.
Ⓖ We can be ________ that our plan was accepted.
Ⓗ You can organize a ________ day to discuss the plan.
Ⓙ They need a ________ way to be fair about the plan.

3. In which sentence is *bias* <u>not</u> used correctly?

Ⓐ Most people have a bias toward their own community.
Ⓑ Students may have a bias against other schools.
Ⓒ Teachers often have a bias toward their own subject.
Ⓓ Pets have a bias that allows them to like everyone.

4. In which sentence could *biased* replace the underlined word or words?

Ⓕ The photo shows an <u>intricate</u> view of the planet Mars.
Ⓖ He prefers this song because he is <u>not equal</u> in his choices.
Ⓗ The CD includes <u>loud and strong</u> music that many people like.
Ⓙ We saw the play and were <u>not excited</u> by the lead actors.

Writing Describe a situation in which *bias* can be a good thing. Be sure to use the word *bias* in your writing.

___

___

___

___

speculate

DAY 1

(verb) To wonder or guess about something without knowing all the facts.

*I can only **speculate** on my grade until I get my score.*

speculation

DAY 2

(noun) A conclusion that is reached by wondering and guessing without all the facts.

*There is **speculation** about who will be chosen for the team.*

hypothesize • hypothesis

DAY 3

hypothesize

(verb) To make a guess based on some knowledge.

*We can **hypothesize** that the rock will fall faster than the feather.*

---

hypothesis

(noun) A prediction or guess based on some knowledge.

*Our **hypothesis** is that the rock will fall faster than the feather.*

theory

DAY 4

(noun) A proposed explanation of something.

*The global warming **theory** explains how the Earth's temperature is rising.*

Day 1 speculate

1. **How would you complete this sentence? Say it aloud to a partner.**

   My friends and I often speculate about ________.

2. **Which word does not provide a clue to the meaning of *speculate*? Circle your answer.**

   a. question c. assume
   b. guess d. exclaim

3. **If you *speculate* about when the school picnic will be, which of these is true? Circle your answer.**

   a. You don't care about the picnic.
   b. You guess different days that the picnic will be held.
   c. You don't know if you want to go to the picnic.
   d. You know when the picnic will be, but you must keep it a secret.

4. **What do you *speculate* the next school year will be like?**

____

____

Day 2 speculation

1. **How would you complete this sentence? Say it aloud to a partner.**

   There is always speculation about ________ in our class.

2. **There is *speculation* that a movie will be filmed in your community. What does that mean? Circle your answer.**

   a. You should start looking for movie stars in your community.
   b. People in your community are not sure they like movies.
   c. Some people think that a movie will be filmed in your community.
   d. Everyone knows for sure that a movie will be filmed in your community.

3. **Which word is not a synonym for *speculation*? Circle your answer.**

   a. assumption c. guess
   b. rumor d. selection

Day 3 hypothesize • hypothesis

1. How would you complete these sentences? Say them aloud to a partner.

I hypothesize that my best friend will ________ as an adult.

To prove a hypothesis, I would need to ________.

2. Which sentence describes what you do when you *hypothesize*? Circle your answer.

a. Make a careful prediction.
b. Make a random guess.
c. Look for a large size in something.
d. Ask your teacher the answer.

3. Which statement does <u>not</u> describe a *hypothesis*? Circle your answer.

a. It can be tested to determine if it is correct.
b. It is known by everyone to be correct.
c. It is a kind of prediction.
d. It can proven true or false.

4. What do you *hypothesize* your future career will be? Why do you make that *hypothesis*?

____

____

____

Day 4 theory

1. How would you complete this sentence? Say it aloud to a partner.

I have heard of the scientific theory that explains ________.

2. What do scientists do to come up with *theories*? Circle your answer.

a. propose to people
b. guess reasons for things
c. perform experiments
d. explain why there are theories

3. What do you think the *theory* of flight does?

____

____

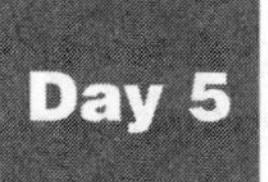
Day 5

speculate • speculation
hypothesize • hypothesis • theory

Fill in the bubble next to the correct answer.

1. In which sentence could *speculate* replace the underlined word?

Ⓐ We can rotate so that everyone gets to go first.
Ⓑ The doctor will operate the first thing in the morning.
Ⓒ The students all wonder about the first day of school.
Ⓓ They will conduct the first tours of the new museum.

2. In which sentence could *speculation* fill in the blank?

Ⓕ The ________ will take place in the morning.
Ⓖ The ________ is in charge of the new activities.
Ⓗ There will be ________ for all students who would like it.
Ⓙ There is ________ that a new coach will be introduced.

3. In which sentence is *hypothesize* used correctly?

Ⓐ It is not likely that someone could hypothesize me.
Ⓑ The doctor can only hypothesize about the problem.
Ⓒ Their hypothesize does not sound accurate.
Ⓓ We will know better when the hypothesize is tested.

4. Which word gives a clue to the meaning of *theory*?

Ⓕ explanation
Ⓖ guess
Ⓗ clue
Ⓙ answer

Writing Describe a *hypothesis* that you could make about homework for tonight. Use at least one of this week's words in your writing.

____

____

____

____

occasional • occasionally DAY 1

occasional

(adj.) Happening from time to time. *We have an **occasional** assembly at school.*

occasionally

(adv.) From time to time. *We **occasionally** get to hear the chorus and band perform.*

intermittent DAY 2

(adj.) Starting and stopping; not happening at regular times. *The school has visiting authors who work with students on an **intermittent** basis.*

continuous DAY 3

(adj.) Going on without stopping. *Many people believe that learning should be **continuous** all through life.*

persistent DAY 4

(adj.) Lasting for a long time. *There is a **persistent** smell in the science lab that should be checked.*

(adj.) Refusing to give up or let go despite many challenges. *He is **persistent** and determined to succeed.*

Day 1 occasional • occasionally

1. How would you complete these sentences? Say them aloud to a partner.

________ is an occasional activity that my family enjoys.

I see ________ occasionally but wish it were more often.

2. Which statement describes an *occasional* event? Circle your answer.

a. It never happens.
b. It has happened once in the past.
c. It happens now and then.
d. It happens every day.

3. Which phrase offers a clue to the meaning of *occasionally*? Circle your answer.

a. once in a while
b. once upon a time
c. one to one
d. once and for all

Day 2 intermittent

1. How would you complete this sentence? Say it aloud to a partner.

________ is an intermittent activity for me because ________.

2. Which of these is true of an *intermittent* problem? Circle your answer.

a. There is no pattern to when it occurs.
b. It is impossible to solve.
c. You get plenty of warning about the problem.
d. It never comes back once you solve it.

3. If a cellphone provides *intermittent* service, which of these is true? Circle your answer.

a. It works all the time.
b. It works some times but not other times.
c. It works every day for the same number of hours.
d. It works whenever you make a call.

4. If someone has *intermittent* pain in his knees, when does it occur?

____

____

____

Day 3 continuous

1. How would you complete this sentence? Say it aloud to a partner.

I have a continuous desire to ________.

2. Which words are synonyms for *continuous*? Circle your answers.

a. nonstop
b. onward
c. constant
d. various

3. A teacher tells students to make a *continuous* effort to improve their writing skills. What does that mean? Circle your answer.

a. Students should do a few writing assignments during the year.
b. Students must write every second of the day.
c. Students should always be working to improve their skills.
d. Students should give up on trying to write anything.

Day 4 persistent

1. How would you complete these sentences? Say them aloud to a partner.

A persistent problem that some students have in school is ________.

I need to be persistent in order to ________.

2. If you have a *persistent* headache, which of these is true? Circle your answer.

a. It won't go away.
b. It lasts for a very short time.
c. You hardly notice it.
d. It helps you think.

3. Your parent says that if you are *persistent,* you will find a way to go to college. What does that mean? Circle your answer.

a. Your parent has hidden money for you to find.
b. You should keep trying to find a way and not give up.
c. You should not bother trying to go to college.
d. You don't know where you want to go to college.

4. Describe a situation in which you were *persistent*.

____

____

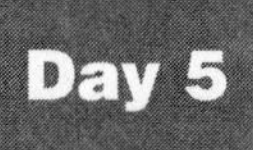

occasional • occasionally • intermittent continuous • persistent

Fill in the bubble next to the correct answer.

1. Which pair of words means the opposite of *occasional* and *occasionally*?

- Ⓐ seldom—never
- Ⓑ frequent—frequently
- Ⓒ rare—rarely
- Ⓓ ever—forever

2. In which sentence is *intermittent* used correctly?

- Ⓕ The lost boat sent an intermittent signal that would start and stop.
- Ⓖ The intermittent players were in every game.
- Ⓗ That song is intermittent on the radio and played all the time.
- Ⓙ The team has an intermittent schedule so they can plan ahead.

I show up **occasionally** in your lessons.

3. In which sentence could *continuous* fill in the blank?

- Ⓐ There are ________ people who can help.
- Ⓑ The children will volunteer for a ________ day.
- Ⓒ We will need a ________ bus to carry everyone.
- Ⓓ They have a ________ need for volunteers.

4. In which sentence could *persistent* replace the underlined words?

- Ⓕ We are the best of friends.
- Ⓖ The sound is going on and on and very loud.
- Ⓗ He is full of fun and makes us laugh.
- Ⓙ They saw a long and boring movie together.

Writing When you have an obstacle to overcome, what helps you to be *persistent?* Be sure to use the word *persistent* in your writing.

____

____

____

____

probable
DAY 1

(adj.) Likely to happen or be true.

*The **probable** outcome of the race will be a win for our team.*

plausible
DAY 2

(adj.) Believable; likely, but not certain, to be true.

*She gave a **plausible** excuse for not attending the ceremony.*

feasible
DAY 3

(adj.) Capable of being done or brought about.

*Finishing the project this week is a **feasible** objective.*

potential
DAY 4

(adj.) Able to come into being; possible.

*The negotiators tried to avoid **potential** conflict between the two countries.*

Day 1 probable

1. How would you complete this sentence? Say it aloud to a partner.

It is probable that my friends and I will ________ this week.

2. It is *probable* that a planned activity will be canceled because of bad weather. What does that mean? Circle your answer.

a. There will be bad weather every day.
b. There are too many activities planned and some should be canceled.
c. An activity may happen that should be canceled.
d. Most likely an activity will not happen because of weather.

3. If the *probable* cause of a fire was grease spilled on a stove, which of these is true? Circle your answer.

a. Everyone agrees that spilled grease caused the fire for sure.
b. The evidence points to a fire caused by spilled grease.
c. No one has an idea about how the fire started.
d. No one is sure if grease can catch on fire.

Day 2 plausible

1. How would you complete this sentence? Say it aloud to a partner.

It is plausible that I can accomplish ________ by the end of this year.

2. Scientists disagree about whether a particular theory is *plausible.* What are they disagreeing about? Circle your answer.

a. if the theory exists
b. if the theory could be true
c. if anyone knows about the theory
d. if anyone cares about the theory

3. Which statement is true of a *plausible* explanation? Circle your answer.

a. It cannot be understood or believed.
b. No one agrees with it.
c. It is full of errors.
d. It is reasonable and can be believed.

Day 3 feasible

1. How would you complete this sentence? Say it aloud to a partner.

A feasible project to complete in a weekend is ________.

2. Which of these is a *feasible* job for a person your age? Circle your answer.

a. caring for a pet
b. performing surgery
c. teaching high school
d. running a company

3. In which sentence is *feasible* not used correctly? Circle your answer.

a. A feasible field trip is to visit the art museum two blocks away.
b. A feasible homework assignment is to write a book by tomorrow.
c. A feasible expectation of students is for them to try their very best.
d. A feasible way to get exercise is to join a sports team.

4. Describe a *feasible* goal you can accomplish this summer.

____

____

Day 4 potential

1. How would you complete this sentence? Say it aloud to a partner.

A potential goal I can accomplish this year is ________.

2. Which statements are not true of a *potential* activity? Circle your answers.

a. It cannot happen.
b. It could happen.
c. It might happen.
d. It will definitely happen.

3. In which sentence is *potential* used correctly? Circle your answer.

a. The potential event will definitely occur.
b. A potential result of the experiment is that the magnet will attract the nail.
c. The student has a potential that she will add to the discussion.
d. Some potentials will affect the outcome of the election.

Day 5 probable • plausible • feasible • potential

Fill in the bubble next to the correct answer.

1. In which sentence is *probable* used correctly?

Ⓐ My probable summer vacation is over.
Ⓑ A probable meeting took place yesterday.
Ⓒ Our probable favorite activity is soccer.
Ⓓ A probable reason for the delay is the rain.

2. Which phrase is a clue to the meaning of *plausible*?

Ⓕ won't happen
Ⓖ not likely to happen
Ⓗ can imagine it happening
Ⓙ it will happen

3. In which sentence is *feasible* used correctly?

Ⓐ He was feasible that he could do it.
Ⓑ It's not feasible to build the model in two days.
Ⓒ No one knows what will happen in the feasible.
Ⓓ Humor is a feasible of this author's writing.

4. In which sentence could *potential* fill in the blank?

Ⓕ We know the ________ party will take place.
Ⓖ The ________ thunderstorm caused flooding.
Ⓗ The bad weather may be a ________ problem.
Ⓙ It is ________ and unusual to see them here.

Writing Explain the difference between a *probable* cause and a *plausible* cause of an accident. Be sure to use the words *probable* and *plausible* in your writing.

____

____

____

____

cite
DAY 1

(verb) To refer to for explanation or proof.

*I always **cite** the sources that I use in my reports.*

citation
DAY 2

(noun) A short note recognizing a source of information or of a quoted passage.

*The **citation** of the history book informed the reader where the writer found her information.*

assert
DAY 3

(verb) To state or declare strongly.

*We need to **assert** our support of our friend.*

validate
DAY 4

(verb) To prove true or factual; to confirm by giving evidence or support.

*The research I found **validates** my idea.*

Day 1 cite

1. How would you complete this sentence? Say it aloud to a partner.

Some references that I might cite for a report are ________.

2. Which statement is true when you *cite* a source? Circle your answer.

a. You give credit to someone else's ideas.
b. You are repeating a rumor.
c. You don't believe the information is worth repeating.
d. You can't see the source's point of view.

3. Which sentence describes someone *citing* a source? Circle your answer.

a. Renita asked her teacher to repeat the directions.
b. Chloe did not write down the author and title of the article in which she found the data.
c. Gavin told his audience who said the quotation he repeated.
d. Tayshaun read an article from the encyclopedia.

Day 2 citation

1. How would you complete this sentence? Say it aloud to a partner.

A citation of a newspaper article would probably include ________.

2. Which sentence uses *citation* correctly? Circle your answer.

a. William always citations his sources.
b. Scott's citation told us where to meet him for the study group.
c. My citation is that you should always give credit to other authors.
d. Emily's essay failed to list several important citations.

3. Why do you think there is so much emphasis on including *citations* in your writing?

____

____

____

____

Day 3 assert

1. How would you complete this sentence? Say it aloud to a partner.

I assert my opinion when ________.

2. In history, you read about a colony trying to *assert* its independence. What does that mean? Circle your answer.

a. The colony is trying to avoid becoming independent.
b. The colony is losing a war for independence.
c. The colony is declaring its right to be independent.
d. The colony is a place where people can be free.

3. If you *assert* your point of view on a topic, which of these is true? Circle your answer.

a. No one knows what you think about the topic.
b. You are not interested in the topic.
c. You don't really have a point of view.
d. Others know exactly what you think about the topic.

4. Why is it important to *assert* your opinions?

____

____

Day 4 validate

1. How would you complete this sentence? Say it aloud to a partner.

I could validate my view on an issue by ________.

2. Which of these things would *validate* global warming? Circle your answer.

a. Statistics and evidence that show an increase in the temperature of the Earth.
b. Statistics and evidence that show a decrease in the temperature of the Earth.
c. A famous person saying he or she believes in global warming.
d. People talking about how it feels warmer this year than last year.

3. Which sentence correctly uses *validate*? Circle your answer.

a. You should validate your thoughts with mine.
b. In order to validate my theory, I disproved it.
c. The experiment should validate the idea that exercise lowers blood pressure.
d. What kind of validate do I need to support my views?

Day 5 cite • citation • assert • validate

Fill in the bubble next to the correct answer.

1. In which sentence is *cite* used correctly?

Ⓐ Find the cite of the restaurant on the map.

Ⓑ We have no way to cite which is the best restaurant to try.

Ⓒ We can call this restaurant to cite what kind of food they serve.

Ⓓ We can cite this restaurant as an example of a good place to eat.

2. In which sentence is *citation* used correctly?

Ⓕ I can citation several reviews that say the movie is awful.

Ⓖ Please include a citation to support your argument.

Ⓗ There is no way to citation how this book will end.

Ⓙ We can citation a famous quote to introduce our presentation.

3. In which sentence could *assert* fill in the blank?

Ⓐ We ________ that we need more time to complete the project.

Ⓑ The ________ of his painting was excellent.

Ⓒ They need an ________ to prove their experiment can work.

Ⓓ We shyly ________ our question to the teacher.

4. Which word is a clue to the meaning of *validate*?

Ⓕ give

Ⓖ support

Ⓗ write

Ⓙ find

Writing What could you use to *validate* your opinion on the necessity of doing well in school? Use at least one of this week's words in your writing.

___

___

___

___

explicit

DAY 1

(adj.) Very clearly stated; precise.

*We received **explicit** instructions for the assignment.*

implicit

DAY 2

(adj.) Not stated but understood in what is said; implied.

*It was **implicit** from the instructions that the assignment was important and should be done carefully.*

denotation

DAY 3

(noun) The most specific, exact meaning of a word or expression.

*The **denotation** of the word "school" is a place where students are taught.*

connotation

DAY 4

(noun) An additional meaning associated with or suggested by a word besides the exact meaning.

*For many students, the **connotation** of "school" is the place where they see their friends.*

Day 1 explicit

1. How would you complete this sentence? Say it aloud to a partner.

An explicit request that I might hear from a teacher is ________.

2. If your parent asks you to be more *explicit* about your plans with friends, what do you need to do? Circle your answer.

a. Don't go into so much detail.
b. State more clearly what you plan to do.
c. Give a reason why you have plans.
d. Explain why you like to be with friends.

3. Which word is not a clue to the meaning of *explicit?* Circle your answer.

a. detailed
b. specific
c. precise
d. unclear

4. Give *explicit* directions from the classroom door to your desk.

____

____

Day 2 implicit

1. How would you complete this sentence? Say it aloud to a partner.

An implicit message that kids can get from adults is ________.

2. Your history teacher asks what is *implicit* when taking a test. How could you respond? Circle your answers.

a. You are to copy the answers from another student.
b. You are to talk during the test.
c. You are to write legibly.
d. You are to do your own work.

3. Which word is a clue to the meaning of *implicit?* Circle your answer.

a. imitated
b. implied
c. important
d. intended

Day 3 denotation

1. How would you complete this sentence? Say it aloud to a partner.

The denotation of the saying "Don't judge a book by its cover" is ________.

2. A test question gives a word and asks you to choose the *denotation*. What do you need to do? Circle your answer.

a. Choose a picture of the word.
b. Choose a sentence using the word.
c. Choose the exact definition of the word.
d. Choose what the word reminds you of.

3. Which statement would be true of the *denotation* of an expression? Circle your answer.

a. It is the precise meaning of the expression.
b. It is the common way some people use the expression.
c. It is finding a new way to use the expression.
d. It is describing the experience of using the expression.

4. Why should you learn the *denotation* of words?

____

____

Day 4 connotation

1. How would you complete this sentence? Say it aloud to a partner.

The connotation of the saying "Don't judge a book by its cover" is ________.

2. If a science teacher asks students to explain their *connotation* of the word "science," which of these is <u>not</u> true? Circle your answer.

a. The teacher wants to find out if students can define "science."
b. The teacher wants to find out how students feel about science.
c. The teacher is checking for activities students connect with science.
d. The teacher is checking for ideas students associate with science.

3. Which of these do you get from the *connotation* of a word? Circle your answer.

a. the exact meaning
b. the proper use of the word
c. what the word suggests
d. how the word is pronounced

Day 5 explicit • implicit • denotation • connotation

Fill in the bubble next to the correct answer.

1. Which word is a synonym for *explicit?*

Ⓐ exciting
Ⓑ sharp
Ⓒ precise
Ⓓ successful

2. In which sentence is *implicit* used correctly?

Ⓕ The implicit message was stated very clearly.
Ⓖ It was implicit by her tone of voice that she was pleased.
Ⓗ If you implicit your feelings, I will understand them better.
Ⓙ No one understands their implicit vocabulary.

3. In which sentence could *denotation* fill in the blank?

Ⓐ The ________ of the word is easy to find with the right resource.
Ⓑ We will need music to ________ the meaning of this word.
Ⓒ There is a ________ of several words to consider when you edit.
Ⓓ There is no need to ________ that word for this assignment.

4. In which sentence is *connotation* not used correctly?

Ⓕ His connotation of "friend" is different from mine.
Ⓖ My connotation of "fun" is not this kind of activity.
Ⓗ Let's check the dictionary for the connotation of "freedom."
Ⓙ Our connotation of a word is influenced by personal experiences.

Writing Explain your *connotation* of the expression "way to go." How is that different from its *denotation?* Be sure to use at least one of this week's words in your writing.

____

____

____

____

relevant • irrelevant DAY 1

relevant

(adj.) Having to do with what is currently being discussed or is important.

*Knowing the last day of school is **relevant** to making our summer vacation plans.*

---

irrelevant

(adj.) Not having to do with what is being considered or discussed.

*The date of winter break is **irrelevant** to making our summer plans.*

appropriate DAY 2

(adj.) Suitable, or right for the purpose.

*It is **appropriate** that all students who made an extra effort should receive an award.*

pertain DAY 3

(verb) To relate to or have to do with something.

*Those materials all **pertain** to geometry.*

pertinent DAY 4

(adj.) Having to do with or connected to a subject.

*That book is **pertinent** to our discussion of books to read this summer.*

Day 1 relevant • irrelevant

1. How would you complete these sentences? Say them aloud to a partner.

Something that is relevant to doing well in school is ________.

Something that is irrelevant to doing well in school is ________.

2. A teacher asks you to choose a *relevant* topic for a report. What does that mean? Circle your answer.

a. You can choose any topic you like.
b. The topic needs to relate to what you are studying.
c. The topic needs to require a lot of research.
d. Everyone is supposed to choose the same topic.

3. A teacher says that your report has *irrelevant* information. What does that mean? Circle your answer.

a. Everything you included in your report is important.
b. You included interesting information in your report.
c. You didn't do as much research as your teacher requested.
d. You included information that is not connected to your topic.

Day 2 appropriate

1. How would you complete this sentence? Say it aloud to a partner.

An appropriate way to treat a new student in school is to ________.

2. If a movie is *appropriate* for all ages, which of these is true? Circle your answer.

a. Only children can see it.
b. Only adults can see it.
c. The movie is suitable for anyone to see.
d. The movie is about people of all ages.

3. Your teacher praises the class because everyone has the *appropriate* materials for an activity. What does that mean? Circle your answer.

a. Everyone has the right materials for the activity.
b. Everyone has done a great job on the activity.
c. Everyone has the oldest materials they could find.
d. Everyone has exciting materials to share.

Day 3 pertain

1. How would you complete this sentence? Say it aloud to a partner.

My favorite kinds of books pertain to ________.

2. Your teacher says that test questions will *pertain* to stories you have read this year. What does that mean? Circle your answer.

a. The test questions will cover many subjects.
b. The test questions will be about stories you have read.
c. The test will have stories to read and questions to answer.
d. You cannot study for the test.

3. If most of your summer activities *pertain* to being outdoors, which of these is true? Circle your answer.

a. You don't care where you are in the summer.
b. You spend a lot of time indoors in the summer.
c. You like to read about and watch different summer activities.
d. Your summer activities primarily take place outside.

Day 4 pertinent

1. How would you complete this sentence? Say it aloud to a partner.

Something that is pertinent to preparing for my future education is ________.

2. Which word is a clue to the meaning of *pertinent*? Circle your answer.

a. related
b. determined
c. indifferent
d. separate

3. Which statement is true of a *pertinent* question? Circle your answer.

a. It is a trick question and has no answer.
b. It is a rude question.
c. It has to do with what is being studied or discussed.
d. It has to do with a topic that should not be discussed.

4. Why would it be important to have *pertinent* resources when you are writing a report?

____

____

relevant • irrelevant • appropriate pertain • pertinent

Fill in the bubble next to the correct answer.

1. Which phrase is a clue to the meaning of *irrelevant?*

Ⓐ point of view
Ⓑ not to the point
Ⓒ to the point
Ⓓ point out

2. Which phrase means the opposite of *appropriate?*

Ⓕ out of place
Ⓖ out loud
Ⓗ up and down
Ⓙ suitable to

3. In which sentence could *pertain* fill in the blank?

Ⓐ The letters do not ________ a large folder to hold them.
Ⓑ The letters ________ many adventures.
Ⓒ The letters ________ ideas that we can discuss.
Ⓓ The letters ________ to our report on famous diarists.

4. Which sentence uses *pertinent* correctly?

Ⓕ A pertinent problem is connected to a situation and needs to be solved.
Ⓖ A pertinent answer has nothing to do with the question that was asked.
Ⓗ A pertinent discussion is not connected to any subject.
Ⓙ A pertinent activity is just for fun and can be done anytime.

Writing Think of a question you have that is *relevant* to what you are studying in school. Where can you find answers that *pertain* to your question? Be sure to use at least one of this week's words in your response.

____

____

____

____

REVIEW: Weeks 28–35

asserted	connotation	feasible	inherent	occasionally	relevant
continuous	hypothesis	integrated	persistent	speculate	

Day 1

Fill in the blanks with words from the word box.

Tenzing Norgay was certain of one thing while he was growing up. Someday, the sherpa would stand on the top of Mt. Everest! Most people didn't believe it ____________________ to climb to 29,028 feet above sea level. But besides being born with ____________________ courage and determination, Tenzing was ____________________. It wasn't until his seventh try that he succeeded in climbing Mt. Everest! On May 29, 1953, he and Edmund Hillary were the first people to stand at the top of the tallest mountain in the world. Although a "sherpa" is still known as a cultural group in Nepal, the word has another ____________________ today—a mountain climber!

Day 2

Fill in the blanks with words from the word box.

Mr. Johnson asked us for questions ____________________ to science. After Lupe asked why the sky looks blue, Mr. Johnson asked us to ____________________ on her question. I guessed that it had to do with light moving through air. Joe had a ____________________ that was more specific. He ____________________ that light appears white but is really several ____________________ colors. It usually moves in a straight and ____________________ line. But ____________________ it bumps into a bit of dust or gas. Then the light bounces off and breaks into individual colors. Blue is simply the color we see most.

REVIEW: Weeks 28–35

appropriate	implicit	objective	potential	speculation
explicit	integral	pertinent	probable	subjective

Day 3

Fill in the blanks with words from the word box.

If you see paper dragons and red decorations in late January or early February, it is ____________________ that they are for Chinese New Year. This holiday is an ____________________ part of Chinese culture. It is an ____________________ time to shoot off fireworks and eat special foods. Some think the holiday began to celebrate the start of spring. Another ____________________ of folklore is that an aggressive beast chased people every new year. People used the color red and fireworks to scare it away. Of course, that explanation is ____________________, as opposed to factual. No matter the reason, though, it's an exciting time of the year!

Day 4

Fill in the blanks with words from the word box.

Before Ms. Diaz left, she gave clear and ____________________ directions to write a paragraph for each question on the board. Those directions eliminated ____________________ questions. She didn't have to remind the students to do their best, either. It was ____________________ every time she assigned a task. When the students came to the final question, they were surprised because it wasn't very factual or ____________________. It was, "What is the most beautiful dessert?" Usually the questions were ____________________ to geography. When Ms. Diaz returned, she looked at the board, started laughing, and exclaimed, "I guess even teachers make mistakes!" She meant to write "desert," not "dessert"!

Day 5

Crack the Code!

Write one of the words from the word box on the lines next to each clue.

appropriate	**continuous**	**integral**	**occasionally**	**relevant**
assert	**denotation**	**integrate**	**persistent**	**speculate**
assertion	**explicit**	**integration**	**pertain**	**speculation**
bias	**hypothesis**	**intermittent**	**pertinent**	**subjective**
biased	**hypothesize**	**irrelevant**	**plausible**	**theory**
cite	**implicit**	**objective**	**possible**	**validate**
connotation	**inherent**	**occasional**	**probable**	

1. stopping and starting ___ ___ ___ ___ ___ ___ ___ ___ ___ ___ ___ ___ (letter 7 = 1)

2. happening from time to time ___ ___ ___ ___ ___ ___ ___ ___ ___ ___ (letter 3 = 2)

3. believable ___ ___ ___ ___ ___ ___ ___ ___ ___ (letter 4 = 3, letter 7 = 4)

4. to refer to for explanation or proof ___ ___ ___ ___ (letter 3 = 5)

5. to have to do with ___ ___ ___ ___ ___ ___ ___ (letter 3 = 6)

6. the exact meaning of a word or an expression ___ ___ ___ ___ ___ ___ ___ ___ ___ ___ (letter 2 = 7)

7. to prove true or factual ___ ___ ___ ___ ___ ___ ___ ___ (letter 2 = 8)

8. a strong feeling that does not let someone be fair ___ ___ ___ ___ (letter 4 = 9)

Now use the numbers under the letters to crack the code. Write the letters on the lines below. The words will answer this question:

Why did George Mallory say he wanted to climb Mt. Everest in 1924?

"___ ___ ___ ___ ___ ___ ___   ___ ___   ___ ___   ___ h ___ ___ ___."

4 7 2 8 3 9 7   1 5   1 9   5 _ 7 6 7

